No.
2. Representative American Speeces:
1948-1949. A. C. Baird. $1.75.

Volume XX

No.
5. Federal World Government. J. E.
Johnsen. $1.50.
6. Federal Information Controls in
Peacetime. R. E. Summers.
$1.50.

No.
7. Should the Communist Party Be
Outlawed? J. E. Johnsen. $1.50.

Volume XIX

No.
3. Free Medical Care. C. A. Peters.
$1.25.

No.
5. United Nations or World Government. J. E. Johnsen. 75c.

Volume XVIII

No.
3. Representative American Speeches:
1945-1946. A. C. Baird. $1.25.
5. Anatomy of Racial Intolerance.
G. B. de Huszar. $1.25.

No.
6. Palestine: Jewish Homeland? J. E.
Johnsen. $1.25

Volume XVII

No.
4. Representative American Speeches:
1943-1944. A. C. Baird. $1.25.

Volume XVI

No.
1. Representative American Speeches:
1941-1942. A. C. Baird. $1.25.

No.
6. Representative American Speeches:
1942-1943. A. C. Baird. $1.25.

Volume XV

No.
1. Representative American Speeches:
1940-1941. A. C. Baird. $1.25.
2. Universal Military Service. R. E.
Summers and H. B. Summers.
$1.25.
3 Federal Regulation of Labor
Unions. J. V. Garland. $1.25.

No.
7. The Closed Shop. J. E. Johnsen.
$1.25.
9. Permanent Price Control Policy.
J. E. Johnsen. $1.25.
10. A Federal Sales Tax. E. R.
Nichols. $1.25.

THE REFERENCE SHELF

Vol. 26   No. 2

FREEDOM AND LOYALTY
IN OUR COLLEGES

Edited by
ROBERT E. SUMMERS
Assistant Professor of Journalism
University of Oregon

THE H. W. WILSON COMPANY
NEW YORK   1954

PREFACE

This volume deals with a unique and generally misunderstood problem: that of the college teacher "suspected" of being a Communist. The problem is unusual in that it involves academic freedom—a freedom not spelled out in the Constitution, but one which has as much meaning and substance for educators as freedom of speech and freedom of the press have for the general public. It is the defense of academic freedom which forms the basis of the present controversy over congressional investigations of the schools, loyalty oaths, and other ramifications of the problem. It is the conflict between the exercise of this freedom and national security measures which gives the issue special significance for a democratic nation.

To many people, the concern of educators and liberals over "rights" of an individual at a time when national survival itself may be in danger seems extremely trivial, if not suspicious. Since this concern on the one hand and suspicion on the other account for much of the misunderstanding and confusion inherent in the present controversy, it is the editor's purpose to try to place the issues into their proper perspective as they relate to the much broader role of American education in an insecure world.

It would be relatively simple if all that were involved were "what to do about the Communist teacher?" Unfortunately, there is much dispute over who or what is a Communist, how he can be found, and what *should* be done with him. And much of the present controversy involves the moral as well as the practical problem of defining a Communist and methods of ferreting him out. This volume is not offered as a solution, but as an effort to give meaning and substance to the issues involved. There is a preponderance of material from the point of view of educators and educational groups. This is to be expected since the educators themselves are most directly concerned, and seek support for their views in the face of widespread public indifference.

For their cooperation and assistance in compiling the material for this volume, the editor wishes to thank Mr. Paul Bixler, Librarian, Antioch College; Mr. Ralph E. Himstead, secretary, American Association of University Professors; Senator William E. Jenner, chairman, Internal Security subcommittee of the Senate Judiciary Committee; Mr. Louis Joughin, research director, American Civil Liberties Union; Dr. A. Blair Knapp, president, Denison University; Mr. William Kostka, Denver (Colorado) public relations executive; and Mr. Karl L. Wagner, state commander, Oregon department, American Legion.

For their kindness in permitting the reproduction of copyrighted materials appearing in these pages, the writer is deeply indebted to the Cornell University Press, the University of Pennsylvania Press, and the University of Washington Press; to the following individuals: Messrs. William F. Buckley, Jr., Emile Caillet, Robert M. MacIver, J. B. Matthews, John Lord O'Brian, Ralph Barton Perry, E. Merrill Root, Norman Thomas, and Dr. Grayson Kirk; to the editors of *AAUP Bulletin, American Mercury, Antioch Review, At Denison, Atlantic Monthly, Bulletin of the Atomic Scientists, Catholic World, Christian Science Monitor, Colorado Alumnus, Commentary, Editorial Research Reports, Freeman, Frontier, Harvard Crimson, Harvard Law Review, Nation, NEA Journal, NEA News, New Leader, New Republic, New York Herald Tribune, New York Times, Ohio State Monthly, Platform (Newsweek), Phi Delta Kappan, Philadelphia Inquirer, Public Affairs Pamphlets, Saturday Review, Social Education, Time, University of Pennsylvania Law Review,* and *Washington University Student Life.*

ROBERT E. SUMMERS
Eugene, Oregon

January 15, 1954

CONTENTS

THE LOYALTY OATH BATTLE

THE FIFTH AMENDMENT CONTROVERSY

COMMUNISM AND NATIONAL SECURITY

EDITOR'S INTRODUCTION

During 1952 and 1953, a continuing procession of educators, mostly college professors, were summoned before congressional committees to testify as to Communist infiltration of the schools and colleges of the nation. This period was characterized likewise by a furor of indignation stemming from liberal organizations, teachers' groups, and many leading educators. But the American public, and even some teachers' groups remained apathetic. Congress generally approved the investigations, and in 1953 voted increased funds to continue the committee inquiries.

The overcharged emotional atmosphere, the political flavor of the charges and countercharges, tended to obscure the main issues. Why should Congress investigate the schools for Communists? Why the increased impetus to find Communists anyway? As Alan Barth pointed out in *The Loyalty of Free Men,* two "tough facts" require acceptance. One is that the Soviet Union today is frankly expansionist and aggressive. The second is that the Communist party of the United States is an instrument of Russian foreign policy. Whether one agrees with either "fact," both have been recognized by the United States Supreme Court in ruling on the constitutionality of the Taft-Hartley Act and on the Communist conspiracy trials. They were also the basis of passage of the Internal Security Act of 1950.

The fact that within the past decade the Soviet Union was an ally, not a probable enemy, and that the American Communist party was an almost respectable and fully legal political party in this country, has tended to further confuse the issue. Now within the space of two or three years, the American Communist has been driven underground, the Communist teacher subjected to intensive investigation by Federal, sometimes state authorities, and generally barred from employment. The ranks of the teaching profession—whether college or the grades—have been split wide open over the stand American teachers should take on the Communist issue. Most of the teachers' organizations were on record until three years ago as favoring the employment and retention of Communist teachers, opposing any discriminatory actions on the part of school administrators to bar any person from the teaching profession for reasons of political or religious belief. Today such a stand would be illegal in many states. And it has been a perplexing question to educational circles as to how to react to the Congressional investigators. Faculties have divided: some factions strongly opposing any investigations; others welcoming investigation as the best means of proving that the schools have nothing to hide.

It may prove helpful to view the question of communism in the colleges as part of a larger problem—that of the Communist threat to our national security. Further, the subject must be considered apart from partisan political implications, apart from "McCarthyism" or the capabilities of Senator Jenner, Representative Velde or their committees. Charges of "communism" in the colleges are nothing new, but they assume a very real and increasing importance in light of the present international situation, since all education is under scrutiny today as to its ability and competence to preserve a democratic America. For this reason, it is important to see the problems of freedom and loyalty in our colleges in their proper perspective, to recognize that they are interrelated to national security, to the full realm of educational philosophy and the public schools of our nation, to individual rights and freedom of the individual, and to the broad principle of academic freedom. To gain this perspective, there are here outlined briefly the developments leading up to the present discussion.

BACKGROUND OF THE LOYALTY ISSUE [1]

Not since the days of the Civil War has the question of loyalty to the American government and our democratic insti-

[1] From *Loyalty in a Democracy,* a round table report edited by Maxwell S. Stewart, editor, Public Affairs Pamphlets. (Public Affairs Pamphlet no 179) Public Affairs Committee. February 1952. p 1-2, 16. Reprinted by permission.

tutions been of such widespread public concern as it is at present. From the earliest days of the Republic the emphasis has been on freedom rather than loyalty. . . . We have always taken the loyalty of most Americans for granted. The number of traitors to the United States has been extremely small throughout our history. We have assumed that the only group to be watched, even in wartime, were those who might owe allegiance to the enemy by reasons of birth. But in recent years the government has set up searching loyalty tests for every one of its employees, including those who boast that their ancestors came over on the Mayflower. Many state and local governments have followed suit. And many private institutions, including schools and colleges, have launched searching loyalty inquiries.

We need not look far for the reason for this sudden concern over the loyalty of our fellow citizens. It is a reflection of growing world tension resulting from the emergence of the Soviet Union as a rival world power. We have seen Communist governments take power in several great nations. And we have become concerned lest in the event of a war between the Communist states and the democracies, the several tens of thousands of Communists in our midst—mostly native-born Americans— might favor the Soviet Union to the extent of traitorous acts against the United States. And since the Communists have sympathizers who have never actually been members of the Communist party, some fear that these sympathizers might be disloyal to the United States.

This fear has been heightened by the Hiss, Remington, and Coplon cases. Alger Hiss, William Remington, and Judith Coplon were all born in the United States. All were well-educated. All held responsible government positions. None had been generally regarded as a Communist or Communist sympathizer. . . .

Many people felt that if these gifted young people, heirs to the finest American tradition, could have betrayed their trust, as they were accused of doing, scores of other government employees, less favored perhaps in training and background, might be disloyal. . . .

The chief fear is, of course, that persons in key government posts may take advantage of their positions to commit acts of espionage or sabotage. But that is not the only fear. Many people are afraid to trust important government decisions to men who are supposed to have "subversive" or unorthodox views. They argue that national policies, particularly in foreign affairs, can be carried out properly only by persons who sympathize entirely with those policies.

The whole problem is complicated by the fact that there is no easy way of detecting potentially "subversive" or disloyal persons. No one will admit disloyalty. Suspicion is heightened by the fact that many Communists keep their party membership secret. The identification of "sympathizers" presents even greater difficulties. Our inability to know who the potential traitors are feeds the fires of distrust. And this distrust, whipped up by fear, has become an important factor in today's political life. . . .

But fright has tended to obscure the real issues. This is evident in the confusion between the quite different problems of security and loyalty. The disclosures regarding atomic spying and the theft of government documents indicate that we have had real reason to be concerned over security. . . . The real problem arises when we seek to determine loyalty which is an attitude, a state of mind. For we are now dealing with an intangible.

The purpose of the President's Loyalty Order, of March 21, 1947, and all loyalty investigations, is to discover in advance if possible all persons who because of wrong attitudes, are likely to commit acts of espionage, sabotage, or treason. This represents a very difficult assignment. . . .

No satisfactory test of a man's loyalty to the United States and its democratic institutions has yet been devised. It is natural that congressional investigating committees and the government's loyalty boards should inquire into the associations of the men they are investigating. When national security is at stake, the investigation may properly include a man's organizational and personal relationships because the test of security is not what a man thinks, what he willingly will do, but beyond that, what he inadvertently will do. . . . But there has been a tendency . . . to regard the associations as the chief evidence. This is probably because the associations seem to provide "tangible" evidence . . . [since] an "association" can be pinned down.

The pinning-down process has been aided by lists of subversive organizations issued by the Attorney General and the various legislative and investigating committees. The practice of making lists of subversive organizations began with the Hatch Act. Originally 6 organizations were listed . . . later, however, . . . somewhat more than 150 organizations were listed by the Attorney General. . . . The House Un-American Activities Committee has issued a list of 694 organizations which it regards as subversive.

NEW ENCROACHMENTS ON
INDIVIDUAL FREEDOM [2]

Chief Justice Hughes once said:

The greater the importance of safeguarding the community from incitements to the overthrow of our institutions by force and violence, the more imperative is the need to preserve inviolate the constitutional rights of free speech, free press and free assembly in order to maintain the opportunity for free political discussion, to the end that government may be responsive to the will of the people and that changes, if desired, may be obtained by peaceful means. Therein lies the security of the Republic, the very foundation of constitutional government.

It is both significant and singular that from the date of the repeal of the Alien and Sedition Laws of 1798 down to 1918 the guarantees of freedom expressed in the First Amendment were accepted without serious question. The Supreme Court had no occasion to interpret the meaning and scope of the First Amendment with reference to seditious utterances of an oral character from the time of its creation until 1919, a period of nearly one hundred and thirty years. Not even the stress and strain of the War between the States gave rise to any court decisions under this amendment. In startling contrast are the numerous occasions since the First World War, and increasingly since the Second World War, on which the power of the

[2] From article by John Lord O'Brian, member of New York and District of Columbia bars, head of War Emergency Division, Department of Justice, 1917-1919. *Harvard Law Review.* 66:2-24. November 1952. Reprinted by permission.

courts has been invoked to limit as well as to protect the liberties of the citizen under the First Amendment. . . .

The emotional excitement engendered in the name of patriotism during a war often persists for long periods after the war is over. Although it originates in the legitimate concerns of patriotism, it usually ends in mass movements in public opinion engendering hatred, bigotry, intolerance for the opinions of others, and, in fact, a desire to suppress the expression of opposing views. . . .

The present problem of maintaining our internal security against subversive influences has been magnified by a fear arising from the novel character of the danger—the infiltration and propaganda by hostile agents and the difficulty of combating that propaganda. Along with this is a feeling that our laws are inadequate and that resort must be had to more ruthless and arbitrary government action. . . .

In appraising the present dangers and the need to resort to new legislation or to alter our traditional policy toward freedom of thought, speech, and association, it may be useful to look to our experience with similar problems in the past. . . .

At the outbreak of the World War in 1914 the people of this nation had had no experience with subversive activities; they had neither realization nor fear of possible enemy activities of this character. The Government likewise was unprepared and had no organizations adequate to cope with such activities. At first foreign propaganda flourished and acts of sabotage were frequent. On and after our entry into the war in 1917, however, precautions taken and laws enforced under the ordinary procedures of civil administration practically eradicated all of these activities. Nevertheless, after the end of the war a wave of public hysteria, to a substantial extent a reaction to earlier events, resulted in conditions of quasi-panic and for a time seriously menaced our basic freedoms, providing an almost exact parallel to what happened in and after World War II. . . .

In . . . 1919 . . . Attorney General Palmer personally planned and directed the so-called Red Raids—"the greatest executive restriction of personal liberty in the history of this country. . . ." These raids took place simultaneously in eleven cities at approximately the same hour on the night of November 7, 1919, and

were followed by similar raids in more than thirty cities on
January 2, 1920. . . . From this time on more sober thought-
fulness began to assert itself and the majority of our people
gradually emerged from the long nightmare of suspicion, distrust, and unreasoned fear. . . .

After 1923 there was uneasiness in some circles with respect
to the activities of the Communist Third International, but the
attitude of the general public was largely negative and indif-
ferent. . . . After the end of [World War II] the change in
the Soviet attitude, the behavior of its leaders, the unconscionable
proof of Russian atrocities shocked the conscience of our nation.
The Congressional Committee on Un-American Activities has
throughout the last dozen years constantly contributed to the
growth of mass emotion by its frequent reports and charges—
many of them justified, but many exaggerated beyond the bounds
of truth. And again, as in 1919 and 1920, there began a sort of
delayed reaction of mass emotion and hysteria which has continued ever since.

Unlike our experience in the first war, however, the new
dangers came in the form of poisonous ideas systematically indoctrinated and secret infiltration by atheistic traitors into un-
suspecting organizations and even into the Government itself.
It was the character of the activities and our inability to understand the Soviet mentality more than the success of their efforts
—indeed, there had been almost no sabotage during the war—
that constantly deepened the sense of apprehension and fear.

The Smith Act. The first change in our traditional attitude
toward freedom of the citizen came in 1940 in a time of grave
national danger: the period of the collapse and surrender of
the French armies. The fear caused by the initial disaster to
the Allies increased to such a point that Congress, on the day
of the enactment of the "Act to Expedite National Defense,"
enacted the Smith Act, which became law on June 28, 1940.
The new law made it unlawful

for any person to organize or help to organize any society, group, or
assembly of persons who teach, advocate, or encourage the overthrow
or destruction of any government in the United States by force or violence; *or to be or become a member of, or affiliate with, any such society, group, or assembly of persons, knowing the purposes thereof.*

Whatever its merits otherwise, Congress had now for the first time made "membership" or "affiliation with" certain subversive organizations a criminal offense. Abhorrent for generations and imported from the Immigration Act of 1918, "guilt by association" became part of the law applicable to citizens.

The Loyalty Order. When hostilities terminated in 1945 the acts of the Soviet government soon provoked a resurgence of anti-Russian suspicion and hostility. The revelations of the Canadian atomic spy case, of treasonable acts within our own Government, and of public confessions by self-confessed traitors greatly intensified the general feeling of apprehension. In new hearings before congressional committees, some of the more conspicuous members publicly urged enactment of more drastic statutes. . . . In the midst of this fresh outburst of agitation, on March 21, 1947, the President promulgated the so-called Loyalty Order, making Government employees subject to dismissal for disloyalty. Subordinate loyalty boards were set up in Government agencies and a board of review of eminent citizens was appointed to hear appeals. Lacking any formal standards for determining loyalty or disloyalty, the members of these various boards inevitably became judges of thought and ideas as well as of conduct and action. They were, in reality, exercising a measure of thought control. . . .

The Loyalty Order also involved drastic departures from traditional procedures. For the first time citizens' rights under the First Amendment of freedom of speech, of thought, and of association were made subject to administrative action. . . .

A final abandonment under the loyalty program of the protection traditionally accorded the individual came in 1951 when the original Executive Order was amended to change the standard for disqualification from "reasonable grounds . . . for belief that the person involved is *disloyal*" to one of "reasonable doubt as to his *loyalty*." The grave effect of this amendment has not yet been fully appreciated: by this change the Anglo-Saxon presumption of innocence is shifted and for all practical purposes the burden is placed upon the individual to prove beyond a reasonable doubt his loyalty and integrity. . . .

The Internal Security Act of 1950. This Act, passed over the President's veto, may well be regarded as a fitting climax to the decade of fear-inspired legislative and executive action which began with the enactment of certain features of the Anti-Subversive Act of 1940. In addition to the well-known provisions requiring registration of "Communist organizations" . . . the statute authorizes the President, acting through the Attorney General, to apprehend and detain in time of national emergency any person, citizen or alien, "as to whom there is reasonable ground to believe that the detainee or possible detainee *probably will* engage in, or *probably will* conspire with others to engage in acts of espionage or of sabotage." In the hearing accorded after detention the Attorney General need establish only probable cause, and judicial review is limited to whether the findings are supported by evidence. Again power has been conferred on administrative officials to deal with our basic liberties of thought, speech, and association. . . .

As has already been stated, prior to World War I the Supreme Court had no occasion to consider . . . the guarantees of freedom contained in the First Amendment. In striking contrast there has been a flood of cases during the past decade in which the Court has been called upon to give consideration to questions under this amendment and other constitutional safeguards of civil liberties. The decisions deal with the rights of aliens, ordinances affecting religious zealots, religion in the schools, governmental employees and others affected by test oaths and loyalty proceedings, legislative investigations and direct restraints upon Communists or others advocating forcible overthrow of the government, and the identification and registration of subversive organizations.

A review of these decisions establishes the disconcerting and perhaps startling fact that in no case has the Court liberalized or extended the freedoms guaranteed by the Constitution. The general trend has been in the direction of sustaining, in the interest of national security, new restrictions upon those liberties. . . .

The same tendency towards acquiescence by the courts is apparent in other areas. . . . The increasing use of publicity by legislative committees to intimidate witnesses and others and to hinder and discourage expression of unpopular views has been held to be beyond the reach of the courts. The doctrine of guilt by association, expressly repudiated only nine years earlier, has apparently been accepted by the Supreme Court. In *Adler* v. *Board of Education* the Court said:

> One's associates, past and present, as well as one's conduct, may properly be considered in determining fitness and loyalty. From time immemorial, one's reputation has been determined in part by the company he keeps.

It is apparent that the Court has, by and large, struggled to uphold legislative or executive action. . . . Underlying this attitude of the Court is, to a large extent, the difficulty of appraising the dangers fear of which has produced the restrictive action. . . . Certainly, the dangers to our political system have increased in recent years, but the degree to which the current state of fear is based on real danger rather than hysteria remains undetermined.

THE BASIS OF FEAR OF SUBVERSION [3]

As a result of evidence adduced before various committees of the Senate and House of Representatives, the Congress hereby finds that—

There exists a world Communist movement which, in its origins, its development, and its present practice, is a world-wide revolutionary movement whose purpose it is, by treachery, deceit, infiltration into other groups (governmental and otherwise), espionage, sabotage, terrorism, and any other means deemed necessary, to establish a Communist totalitarian dictatorship in the countries throughout the world through the medium of a world-wide Communist organization. . . .

The direction and control of the world Communist movement is vested in and exercised by the Communist dictatorship of a foreign country.

The Communist dictatorship of such foreign country . . . establishes . . . in various countries, action organizations which are not free and independent organizations but sections of a world-wide Communist organization and are controlled, directed, and

---

[3] From the text of the Internal Security Act of 1950, Title I—Subversive Activities Control Act of 1950 (*U.S. Code*, supp. IV to 1946 ed., "War and National Defense," ch23, sec781, p2522-3. Superintendent of Documents. Washington 25, D.C. '51.)

subject to the discipline of the Communist dictatorship of such foreign country.

The Communist action organizations so established and utilized in various countries . . . endeavor to carry out the objectives of the world Communist movement by bringing about the overthrow of existing governments by any available means, including force if necessary. . . . Although such organizations usually designate themselves as political parties, they are in fact constituent elements of the world-wide Communist movement and promote the objectives of such movement by conspiratorial and coercive tactics, instead of through democratic processes. . . .

Such Communist organizations in various countries are organized on a secret, conspiratorial basis and operate to a substantial extent through organizations known as "Communist fronts," which in most instances are created and maintained, or used, in such manner as to conceal the facts as to their true character and purposes and their membership. . . .

In the United States those individuals who knowingly and willfully participate in the world Communist movement, when they so participate, in effect repudiate their allegiance to the United States, and in effect transfer their allegiance to the foreign country in which is vested the direction and control of the world Communist movement. . . .

The Communist network in the United States is inspired and controlled in large part by foreign agents. . . .

The Communist movement in the United States is an organization numbering thousands of adherents, rigidly and ruthlessly disciplined. . . . The Communist organization in the United States, pursuing its stated objectives, the recent success of Communist methods in other countries, and the nature and control of the world Communist movement itself, present a clear and present danger to the security of the United States and to the existence of free American institutions, and make it necessary that Congress, in order to provide for the common defense, to preserve the sovereignty of the United States as an independent nation, and to guarantee to each state a republican form of government, enact appropriate legislation recognizing the existence of such world-wide conspiracy and designed to prevent it from accomplishing its purpose in the United States.

ATTACKS OF THE PAST [4]

Current attacks upon the freedom of American schools and universities can best be understood against the background of earlier struggles. In colonial days we had neither religious nor academic freedom. Schools were originally set up to promote the religious views of the dominant element in the community. Religious soundness was the chief criterion of fitness to teach. The first president of Harvard College, for instance, was driven from his post and from the colony when he accepted the Baptist view of infant baptism. As late as the end of the colonial period President Clapp of Yale made the interesting ruling: "Though every man has a right to examine and judge for himself according to truth; yet no man has a right to judge wrong." Teachers, however, were scarce; suppression of heresy proved difficult. In communities that needed more people economic prosperity was promoted by tolerating men of unorthodox, even dangerous views.

The men who founded our nation included freedom of religion among the fundamental freedoms. An established church was abandoned. Gradually, the idea of separation of church and state was accepted. In our early national period advocates of freedom won removal of legal penalties for wrong views and practices even in the field where error was considered most dangerous, provided always that the offender was a Trinitarian Protestant Christian. Legal discrimination against Jews, Catholics, Unitarians, and atheists was also finally abolished. Public schools were protected against control by religious pressure groups.

For a time during the Revolution political as well as religious conformity was required of teachers. All states established test oaths for civil officials; New Jersey had one that applied specifically to teachers. Since a large proportion of the educated people

[4] From "Teacher as Rebel: His War for Freedom," by Howard K. Beale, professor of history, University of Wisconsin. *Nation.* 176:412-14. May 16, 1953. Reprinted by permission.

were loyal to England, a good many teachers were affected. President Cooper of King's College, now Columbia University, not only lost his job but fled half-clad over a fence to a British sloop to escape indignant "patriots."

Then came the French Revolution and the struggle in this country between the Hamiltonian men of property and the Jeffersonians who acclaimed the "French" ideas of liberty and equality. A sedition act passed by the Hamiltonians imposed severe restrictions upon criticism of the government. While the fear of dangerous French ideas was at its height, Harvard dropped its courses in the French language and literature. But in the end those who sought to restrict free speech were overwhelmingly repudiated by the voters. The Jeffersonians repealed the sedition act and reestablished our freedoms. Harvard, after eight years, restored French to the curriculum.

In the mid-nineteenth century slavery became the most bitterly contested issue before the American people. Southern slaveholders were the greatest propertied interest in the country. Northern manufacturers and other men of wealth sympathized with the slaveholders' desire to protect their property. The antislavery agitation threatened not only the property and labor system, but the very social stability of the South. Abolition was as frightening to southern whites as communism is today to Americans in all parts of the country. Southern states made it a crime to teach Negroes. Throughout the South teachers were dismissed and often driven from the community for asserting that to hold men in bondage was wrong. Among them were President Partridge of Mississippi College, Professor Birney of Centre College, and the whole faculty of Berea. At the University of North Carolina Professor Hedrick was dismissed for supporting a subversive organization—the Republican party.

Since Abolitionists were Northerners, the principle of guilt by association made all Northern teachers and books suspect in Southern schools. At one time even Northern schools and colleges suppressed criticism of slavery. Connecticut and New Hampshire mobs attacked schools that accepted Negroes. Miami University, Kenyon College, and Lane Theological Seminary banned student antislavery societies as a subversive. Antislavery professors were dismissed at Lane and Harvard, and Harvard students threw rotten eggs at the college's distinguished alumnus, Ralph Waldo Emerson, when he gave an antislavery lecture. On the other hand, the President of Franklin College was forced out because of his proslavery views. Harvard dismissed Judge Loring from a law lectureship because he had enforced the law and returned a fugitive Negro to the South.

After war broke out, the presidents of Bowdoin and Dartmouth and teachers in many places were dismissed for defending slavery and secession. Then, for fifty years after the war ended, its issues were refought. The United Daughters of the Confederacy in the South, the Grand Army of the Republic in the North attacked teachers and textbooks and tried to replace sound history with the version they preferred. Publishing houses and textbook writers had to put out one kind of history for the South and another for the North.

Meanwhile scientists were making new discoveries and presenting the hypothesis of evolution to the world. In many places teachers who introduced the new knowledge in their classrooms and professors of theology who applied it to their religious teaching were fired: for example, at the Baptist Seminary in Louisville, the Presbyterian Seminary in South Carolina, and at Vanderbilt in Tennessee. The appointment of Harvard's great president, Eliot, was opposed on the ground that a scientist could not maintain sound education; powerful members of the Board of Overseers tried unsuccessfully to prevent Eliot's having John Fiske lecture at Harvard on evolution. At Yale, President Porter conducted a course discrediting Herbert Spencer's evolutionary teachings.

Andrew White, president of Cornell, on the other hand, defended the right of scientists to teach the truth as they saw it. Efforts of religious pressure groups to suppress academic freedom, he warned, did far more harm to religion than to science, "for thereby suspicions are widely spread, especially among open-minded young men, that the accepted Christian system demands a concealment of truth, with the persecution of honest investigators, and must therefore be false." The Women's Christian Temperance Union was powerful enough, however, to force schools all over the country to adopt physiology textbooks containing "scientific" information that medical men denounced as untrue but that these devoted and determined ladies wished inculcated.

In the nineties, with the growth of industrialization, social and economic questions began to cause the most trouble. President Harper at the new University of Chicago stood ready to defend freedom of science and religious teaching but was caught off guard by the demand that he dismiss an economist for criticizing the practices of the Pullman Company, whose founder was one of Chicago's leading citizens. From then until our own day schools and colleges have been under attack for their teachings on race relations, slum clearance, labor problems, security legislation, public ownership or even control of utilities, regulation of industry, and any other social or economic question the community feels strongly about.

In the 1920's religious groups again attacked the teaching of evolution, this time in the lower schools too. Books were banned, or mutilated by having the pages on evolution cut out. Teachers were cowed into avoiding any mention of the doctrine. State laws in Mississippi, Louisiana, and Tennessee forbade its discussion.

An extreme brand of patriotism also took possession of us in those years. The schools were attacked by the American Legion and the D.A.R. Teachers were dismissed for not distorting history "patriotically" to show that Britain had been solely to blame for the American Revolution and our other disagreements with it. Eminent historians, faced with the blacklisting of their books, changed them to please the politicians. In the thirties books were condemned because Catholics or Jews did not like their contents, and the excellent history of an eminent Catholic historian was barred from the New York schools by a Presbyterian superintendent on complaint of an obscure Episcopal clergyman until the author changed certain statements about the Reformation that non-Episcopal Protestant historians regarded as entirely sound.

After World War I a "red scare" developed. Loyalty tests were imposed. Powerful forces sought to brand as "radical" and hence as "disloyal" all unorthodox opinions. In New York, Governor Alfred E. Smith protested that the Lusk laws permitted "one man to place upon any teacher the stigma of disloyalty." "No man," he said, "is so omniscient or wise as to have intrusted to him power not only to condemn any individual teacher but to decree what belief or opinion is opposed to the institutions of the country. . . . Within the limits of the penal law every citizen may speak and teach what he believes." Three years later, when the hysteria had died out, the people of New York repealed the laws setting up the loyalty tests. Sheets like the Hearst papers and the Chicago *Tribune* continued to attack democratic freedoms in the schools and colleges, but as the twenties passed into the thirties fewer and fewer people supported their campaign.

Though the desire of politicians for votes and of newspapers for subscribers has sometimes motivated attacks upon the schools, more often the attackers, like the opponents of abolition and evolution, have sincerely believed they were combating a dangerous development. Their sincerity, however, has not made their threat any less menacing.

COLLEGES AS TARGETS FOR ATTACKS [5]

Academic freedom is under constant attack today from many sources. Attacks upon colleges and universities as centers of radicalism and on professors as "subversive" are not new in this country. Tewksbury, in his study of the establishment of colleges in America before the Civil War, points out that certain Easterners were reluctant to support many of the new frontier institutions because they believed "many colleges in the West were hotbeds of social and economic radicalism."

Over the years in America some suspicion of professors has always existed. In the present period of grave tension and fear, the distrust of professors, and of the colleges and universities where they do their work, has naturally increased. The result

[5] From "An Intellectual Iron Curtain," by Francis H. Horn, executive secretary, Association for Higher Education, National Education Association. *National Education Association Journal*. 42:152-5. March 1953. Reprinted by permission.

has been intensified attacks upon the traditional freedom of institutions of higher education.

Evidence of these attacks is in every day's headlines. Congressional investigators have been concerned with alleged "Red professors" for several years, especially through the House Un-American Activities Committee. A number of states followed the lead of the House with similar committees. The Senate also, through its Judiciary Subcommittee on Internal Security (the Mc-Carran Committee of the Eighty-second Congress) began, somewhat later, to exploit the possibilities of weeding out so-called leftist influences in higher education. Its investigations quickly made the headlines, with charges that "nests of Communists" existed in many colleges.

But according to some congressional leaders these previous investigations have only scratched the surface, and it is implied that deeper digging for leftists will have spectacular results. . . . Representative Velde, . . . chairman of the House Un-American Activities Committee, . . . stated that his committee had a dozen investigators looking into twenty-five colleges. . . .

Senator Joseph McCarthy, . . . chairman of the Senate Committee on Government Operations, . . . proposed getting into the business of exposing . . . not just Communists but "Communist thinkers." What a "Communist thinker" is remains to be determined, but Mr. McCarthy proclaimed that this would prove to be "the most unpopular, the most unpleasant task anyone can do . . . because the minute you do that all hell breaks loose. From coast to coast you hear the screaming of interference with academic freedom." . . .

The Senator's views on such infiltration are indicated in *McCarthyism, the Fight for America,* when he quotes a statement made last spring by the former research director of the House Un-American Activities Committee:

Approximately 28 per cent of all the top collaborators with the deceitful Communist-front movement in recent years have been college and university professors.

Exhaustive research into the personnel of Communist-front organizations reveals that some 3,000 professors from approximately 600 institutions of higher learning have been affiliated more than 26,000 times with these instruments of the Communist party. This is not guilt by association but guilt by collaboration.

Referring to these allegedly Communist-minded teachers, Mr. McCarthy writes, "Academic freedom means their right to force you [the American citizen] to hire them to teach your children a philosophy in which you do not believe." . . .

In addition to facing attacks from these official quarters, institutions of higher learning are being subjected to constant hammering against academic freedom by various individuals and organizations that regard themselves as special guardians of the public welfare. In the forefront of this group is Allen Zoll's unsavory National Council on American Education, which has been a leader in the attacks upon the public schools.

The NCAE is dedicated, its pronouncements say, to "the eradication of Marxism and collectivism from . . . schools and colleges." It is the publisher of the "Red-ucator" pamphlets, which list "Communist" and "subversive" professors at Harvard, Yale, California, Cal Tech, Stanford, and leading women's colleges, with the suggestion that alumni and parents of students take steps to force the institutions to get rid of these "un-American" professors. The NCAE also published *American Higher Education: Its Betrayal of Trust and Faith,* which charges that "academic freedom is the major Communist party line for American higher education."

Similar charges are echoed in scores of American newspapers, led by the Chicago *Tribune.* (It must be remembered, however, that many newspapers, such as the Washington *Post,* the New York *Times,* and the *Christian Science Monitor,* are among the stoutest defenders of academic freedom.)

A number of magazines have also joined the growing denunciation of "Red professors." The *American Legion Magazine* has featured, along with other attacks, "Do the Colleges *Have* To Hire Red Professors?" (by Louis Budenz) which accuses higher institutions of harboring Communists, who are alleged to "cloak themselves in academic freedom."

The *Freeman,* promising "to devote considerable attention to the neglected savannas of higher education," has in recent months published pieces on "Our Left-Handed Professors" and on alleged subversives at Vassar. The *American Mercury,* in "The Treason of the Professors," has provided William F. Buckley, Jr., with a forum from which to continue his attack upon "the superstitions of academic freedom."

It is not only the professors who are under attack, but college administrators charged with protecting the suspected teachers. A West Coast weekly, for example, has called for the dismissal of President Sproul on the grounds that he had so long "dealt with Commies, Red sympathizers, and Red-front organizations."

In addition to such direct attacks upon the traditional freedom of colleges and universities there are a number of other developments threatening academic freedom. These include the proscription of textbooks . . . ; attempts to impose gag rules on speakers appearing on college campuses; and loyalty oaths.

INDICTMENTS AGAINST THE SCHOOLS

EDITOR'S INTRODUCTION

The charges brought against the schools during the past couple of years have not been too numerous or too specific. To a large degree, the attacks have been the same for the past twenty years, but only today have many people given them serious consideration.

Considering the fact that the cry of "Reds in our colleges" has received relatively little publicity outside of the ultra-conservative press, that the charges have come from so few sources and have rarely been echoed by any responsible political leaders or organized groups, it may be difficult to understand why so much furor has developed recently over the issue. Especially does it seem worth noting that most magazines and newspapers have devoted what seems to be an overwhelming amount of space to answering the handful of critics of education.

Several events have taken place which directly affect the present picture. One is that "progressive education" in the lower grades has received much unfavorable attention throughout the nation and the attacks and counter-attacks on public school teaching methods have aroused a more widespread interest in education on the part of the general public. Second, the publication of *God and Man at Yale* by William F. Buckley, Jr., which charged that moral values were not being taught in the colleges, gave impetus to the fears of those who had viewed with alarm the wave of exposures of athletic corruption, cribbing on examinations, and similar evidence of moral decline in the colleges. Third, the rather widespread controversy over draft deferments for college students helped create an understandable antagonism toward the colleges, when even James B. Conant of Harvard found it necessary to say that the Selective Service procedure operated to keep those who could afford to go to college at home, and sent the non-college boy to Korea. It would be improper to dismiss the charges of communism in the colleges as merely "Red-baiting" or "McCarthyism" or even as a rather terrifying but natural outcome of the tensions resulting from the cold war. The combination of recent events involving American education on all levels, plus the cold war tensions, plus the fears and emotions aroused over the Communist spy trials and the disclosures of "subversion" by government investigating committees—all together present a formidable picture. There is great danger of oversimplifying the issues involved, and thereby being unable to understand the impetus of the attack and the reason why many people, including members of college faculties, accept the views of some, if not all, of the critics.

This section, while eliminating the criticisms of the public schools, which are discussed in Sturges F. Cary's *New Challenges to Our Schools* (Reference Shelf, v25, no 1), attempts to round up some of the more significant points of view among the critics of the colleges. These points of view are presented here as representative of the nature and sources of the major charges leveled against American colleges in recent months.

THE KEY ARGUMENTS [1]

The most violent battles of the past year have centered around four specific attacks on the way American schools and colleges have been going about their jobs.

1. They fail to teach the fundamentals. . . . The elementary schools are accused of neglecting the most basic teaching of all—the three R's. The critics mostly blame this failure on the progressive education methods stemming from John Dewey, which, they claim, have coated the learning process with so much sugar that many students never get a firm grasp of anything. . . .

2. They neglect moral and religious values. The critics assign several causes to this field of neglect. One stems from what they feel is a tendency to substitute science for the fundamental virtues, truths and ideals that scholars and teachers followed in the past. Too many present-day educators, in this view, in an eagerness to follow the all-enlightening statistical trail, have let

[1] From "New Crises for Education," study guide. In *Platform*, published by the Newsweek Club and Educational Bureaus. p4-6. January 1952. Reprinted by permission.

the laboratory and the scientist become "the local deities, if not the supreme being in academic life."

At the same time religion as such has been put on short rations. If religion is formally taught at all today, it is not seen in terms of a living faith, but more in the atmosphere of a foreign language or an ancient, possibly somewhat quaint, social history. William F. Buckley, Jr., in his controversial book, *God and Man at Yale* . . . , alleges that the atmosphere predominating in Yale's religion department implies that religion is "at best, a useful superstition," while many teachers look on it as "distinctly harmful benightedness."

Small wonder, the critics hold, that in an ambiance so lacking in faith, students in some of our institutions of learning cheat on examinations, take bribes, use dope and become involved in gambling syndicates.

3. They are producing "citizen-robots." Instead of teaching certain unarguable truths, the trend today, say some of the recent critics, is to show that all values are relative rather than absolute. "We have in this country certain traditions which are not subject to re-examination, that we want to adhere to," was the comment expressed in a recent Northwestern Reviewing Stand broadcast. . . . But the schools are teaching our youth to make their decisions, not in terms of what is right but of what is expedient.

Schools and colleges with this kind of focus make no attempt to awaken a core of individual purposefulness in their students . . . and the inevitable result has been what one critic calls a "moral neutrality," which "like a noxious gas, today pervades every corner of American life."

4. They are seedbeds of collectivism. Complaints on this score fall into several categories. Some educators are accused of belittling American institutions, criticizing free enterprise, debunking long-held traditions. Under the guise of devotion to change, according to this charge, students are taught that the American economic system has led to abuses and unequal benefits.

At the same time that traditional institutions come up for ridicule, according to some, our schools and universities are using the classroom as propaganda centers, instilling in young minds "the absolute value and power of the state." Our universities, wrote Jack Schwartzman in the *Freeman,* "are the training grounds for the barbarians of the future. . . ." Their graduates, he predicts, "in the guise of learning, shall come forth loaded with pitchforks of ignorance and cynicism, and stab and destroy the remnants of human civilization."

Along similar lines of thought, a recent resolution passed by the American Medical Association reads: "Many of our educators and many of the organizations to which they belong have for many years conducted an active, aggressive campaign to indoctrinate their students in grammar school, high school and college with the insidious and destructive tenets of the welfare state, this teaching of hatred and scorn for the American system of private enterprise having been so widespread and successful that as a result our voters are conditioned to accept all manner of totalitarian expedients in direct violation of economic law."

Already, in the eyes of some, old age security, old age pensions, unemployment insurance, wage regulation, price controls, savings bonds and increased taxes stand as dark reminders that America is abandoning the old principles of individualism and idealism. The fact that many students come home and praise this kind of legislation only testifies more strongly to the misguidedness of their teachers and exposes the classroom's part in pushing this country toward socialism.

Another serious charge leveled in this connection is that both schools and colleges are indiscriminately using biased textbooks to instill collectivist ideas, and hiring collectivist-minded teachers to teach such sensitive subjects as economics and politics. "We would be satisfied, as a starter," commented the *Freeman* magazine on this score, "if a good individualist were accorded an equal chance at a job. . . . The real trouble in our universities is not that collectivists have infiltrated our departments of economics and social science; it is that they have largely taken over, and blanketed the individualist opposition."

THE COMMUNIST INFLUENCE IN EDUCATION [2]

The Internal Security Subcommittee received throughout the session considerable evidence of Communist influences at work in the educational process in the United States. The evidence originated in all parts of the country and bore directly on Communist penetration of the nation's colleges, high schools, and elementary schools. . . .

On the basis of the evidence so far adduced, the committee has concluded that:

1. Despite the unquestioned loyalty and self-sacrificing devotion to duty of the preponderant bulk of America's teachers, there are yet many hundreds of teachers who are Communists.

2. Communist teachers radiate an influence much greater than their proportionate number.

3. Their influence has reached out into the community, among youth and parent-teacher organizations and Communist-front groups. . . .

4. A Communist is not a fit person to be placed or retained in a position to influence the minds of the youth of America.

EXTENT OF COMMUNIST INFILTRATION [3]

For more than seventeen years, the Communist party of the United States has put forth every effort to infiltrate the teaching profession of this country. In this endeavor to corrupt the teachers of youth, the agents of the Kremlin have been remarkably successful, especially among the professors in our colleges and universities.

In these few years, the Communist party has enlisted the support of at least 3,500 professors—many of them as dues-paying members, many others as fellow travelers, some as out-and-out espionage agents, some as adherents of the party line in varying degrees, and some as the unwitting dupes of subversion.

[2] From *Subversive Influence in the Educational Process*, report, January 2, 1952, of the McCarran subcommittee to investigate the administration of the Internal Security Act and other internal security laws, to the Senate Judiciary Committee. 82d Congress, 2d session. The Committee. Washington 25, D.C. 1952. p 1, 12-13.
[3] From "Communism and the Colleges," by J. B. Matthews, former staff director, United States Senate subcommittee on investigations. *American Mercury.* 76:111-44. May 1953. Reprinted by permission.

Congressional committees, which are now investigating Communists in the colleges, are on the track of a national scandal. . . .

The ordinary day-to-day work of the Communist party is many-sided, ranging all the way from open propaganda to espionage. In whatever it wanted done, the party has always been able to draw upon members of the academic profession for the running of its subversive apparatus. The intellectual uncertainties and moral chaos of the past quarter of a century have contributed to this achievement of the Kremlin agents in the colleges and universities. . . .

Secret Communist party members among teachers have been estimated at 1,500. . . .

A conservative estimate places at close to 3,500 the number of professors in colleges and universities who have collaborated with the Communist-front apparatus, since its inception about seventeen years ago. They represent every state in the Union and the District of Columbia. They have been connected with some 400 institutions of higher learning. More than a thousand of them have been active collaborators with the Communist-front apparatus since the beginning of Cold War I [Mr. Matthews defines Cold War I as the period of the Berlin airlift, 1948-1949—Ed.]. . . .

The Communist-front organization is just as integral a part of the whole Communist conspiracy as are the Communist party itself, the party press, the party training schools, and party espionage cells. All are directed by a central high command, and all are coordinated to achieve a single end—the overthrow of the United States government by force and violence. . . .

Anyone who supports a Communist-front organization, even by the limited action of lending his name as a sponsor, is supporting the Communist conspiracy whether he knows it or not. If he supports it by speaking, contributing funds, recruiting others, or serving as an official, he is giving active and overt aid to the enemy of the United States. . . . Even if the respectable professor who sponsors a Communist front does not become a Communist party member or an espionage agent himself, he helps to create and maintain an organization through which others become deeply enmeshed in subversion, espionage, and treason. . . .

One of the most influential of the present-day Communist-front organizations is the National Council of the Arts, Sciences and Professions. The congressional Committee on Un-American Activities issued a comprehensive report on the organization, demonstrating its Communist character beyond any possibility of doubt. . . .

On March 25, 1949, this long arm of the Kremlin, the NCASP, convened the Cultural and Scientific Conference for World Peace in the Waldorf-Astoria Hotel in New York City. . . . It should be recalled that the Berlin airlift was almost exactly one year old when the Waldorf-Astoria conference met. There was no longer any reason for intelligent people to doubt that the Soviet Union, its American agents, and their Communist-front apparatus were enemies of the United States. . . .

In view of the subversive nature of the Waldorf-Astoria conference and its parent organization, the NCASP, it is revealing to find the names of seven presidents of institutions of higher learning listed among the sponsors. . . .

Where we do not find active collaboration by professors with the Communist-front movement, we find that the prevailing academic attitude is one of apathy or complete indifference. Any resistance to Moscow on the American campus is likely to come from professors whose ideological outlook is socialistic.

The ACPFB [American Committee for Protection of Foreign Born] is the oldest Communist party auxiliary still functioning in the United States. It was launched in 1924 with the name, National Council for Protection of Foreign Born Workers. Its Communist party parentage was open and above-board. . . .

The 1952 annual meeting of the ACPFB was held in Detroit, December 13-14, under the name of the National Conference to Defend the Rights of Foreign Born Americans. This annual meeting of the ACPFB had the names of eighty-six sponsors printed on its program, of whom thirty-two were college or university professors . . . from twenty-four institutions of higher education in eleven states. . . .

The Committee for Medical Freedom is one of the newest units of the Communist-front apparatus. It lists among its sponsors the names of forty-two professors. . . . Like all units of the

Communist-front apparatus, the Committee for Medical Freedom is on a rampage against legislative investigations of communism. . . .

Of the numerous Communist-front organizations set up to implement Stalin's "peace" movement, one of the largest which claimed the support of the professors was the Mid-Century Conference for Peace. The Mid-Century Conference for Peace met in Chicago, May 29-30, 1950, with 700 delegates attending from all parts of the United States . . . sponsored by more than 350 persons more or less prominent in the fields of education, religion, law, art, writing, and science. Sponsoring the Chicago meeting were 104 professors from sixty-three educational institutions in twenty-eight states. . . .

Thirty-four per cent of the top hundred academic collaborators with the Communist-front apparatus are listed in *American Men of Science,* the great American directory of scientists. . . .

Let it be set down here and never forgotten that the facts about the professors' Communist cells in the Manhattan Engineering District (A-bomb project) were not uncovered by the administrators of the University of California, the University of Minnesota, the University of Puerto Rico, Fisk University, or the Brooklyn Polytechnic Institute. They were uncovered, for the public gaze, by a newspaper, the New York *Journal-American,* and by the congressional Committee on Un-American Activities. . . . So far as we have been able to ascertain, after the most extensive investigation, no college or university administration has turned a little finger to ferret out the Communists on their faculties until after the academic agents of the Kremlin have been exposed by legislative investigations.

Nevertheless and notwithstanding, there are academicians, newspapers, and politicians who take the stupid and untenable position: "Let the colleges and universities themselves do the job." . . .

All the fake liberals and many misguided or fellow-traveling educators take the position that it is a violation of academic freedom to expose Communists on college and university faculties. They hold that it is a violation of "democratic liberties" to dismiss agents of the Kremlin when they are found hiding in teaching positions.

The American Association of University Professors is the largest and most representative body composed exclusively of teachers in colleges and universities. As of this writing, the AAUP takes the following position on the question of employing Communists on the faculties of higher institutions of learning: "So long as the Communist party in the United States is a legal political party, affiliation with that party in and of itself should not be regarded as a justifiable reason for exclusion from the academic profession. . . .

"There is, then, nothing in the nature of the teaching profession which requires the automatic exclusion of Communists, and the attempt to exclude them would threaten our educational system with real dangers. . . ." The generous assumption is that the true nature and aims of the Communist party are not yet understood by the academic profession as a whole. Any other assumption would be to impute a prevalent disloyalty to the teaching force of the country. . . .

Nothing could be more desirable, in the matter of communism on American campuses, than for the colleges and universities of the country to conduct their own investigations into the Communist activities of subversive professors and to take appropriate action when they are exposed. Unnecessary government intervention of any kind anywhere is undesirable in a free society. The undeniable fact, however, is that little or nothing has ever been done to remove any Communist from any faculty anywhere in the United States until the pressure of legislative investigation has been applied. . . . The plain fact of the matter is that college and university administrations are more or less helpless to deal with Communists without the assistance of legislative inquiries. The administrators of higher education do not possess either the power of subpoena or the power to initiate perjury and contempt proceedings, both of which are indispensable when dealing with the conspiratorial agents of a foreign state, who do not hesitate to lie when not faced with a penalty for so doing.

Nevertheless and notwithstanding, there are educators who grow hysterical and abusive over the very suggestion of a legislative investigation of Communists in colleges and universities. They arouse the suspicion, rightly or wrongly, that they are satisfied to have the agents of Moscow operate on American campuses without let or hindrance.

IN DEFENSE OF CRITICISM [4]

Underpaid, underappreciated, and overworked, teachers are compensated by unique powers. They have the power, over the long term, to tailor the society they live in to their own specifications. They exercise this power constantly. Every time a legislature meets, a convention sits, an editorial is written, the teacher tastes the fruits of his own making.

All publicists—politicians, writers, and orators—express views that are midwifed by intellectuals, developed by intellectuals, screened by intellectuals, and, finally, certified by intellectuals. These views are communicated to society through the schools. They thereupon determine the thinking, and hence the activities, of all free societies. . . .

The raging controversy about school policy that has grown bitter in the last few years, and in recent months particularly . . . will continue, and probably it will get more heated.

One point of view is basically as follows:

"Teaching is a highly specialized skill. It takes years of special training. The layman doesn't qualify to instruct the teacher just because he has taken note of casual remarks his son makes at the breakfast table, leafed through an occasional textbook that he uses, or even because he's had an occasional chat with his teacher." . . .

The crux of the matter lies in the educators' receptivity to what they call "responsible" criticism. Who is to decide what is "responsible" and what is "irresponsible" criticism? The educators have covered themselves: They will retain the privilege of distinguishing between the two. . . .

The denunciations of present-day lay critics whose principal grievances center around collectivism, secularism, and "progressive" education in the schools, are dismissed with spirited and categorical denunciations. . . .

[4] From "Freedom to Agree," by William F. Buckley, Jr., author of *God and Man at Yale*. *American Mercury*. 76:101-7. June 1953. Reprinted by permission.

The educational groups do not do all their own pleading. They have been successful in mobilizing a powerful lobby of publicists to help them assert their monopoly on public education. No less than one hundred books, pamphlets, and articles have been published in recent months scoring the critics. And they have appeared in such diverse magazines as the *American Teacher*, the *Nation*, the *American Scholar*, the *Reporter*, the New York *Times Book Review, School and Society,* the *Arkansas Journal*, the *Christian Century, Commentary*, the *Saturday Review of Literature*, and *McCall's*. . . .

And so we have it: Lay critics of the drift of modern education are "unjust," "insincere," "hypocritical," or a well-proportioned blend of all three; at best, they are "unknowing." . . .

The basis of most of the attacks on the drift of modern education is that the schools, or many of them at least, are promoting collectivism and secularism. As far as most educators are concerned, these charges are easily and automatically reducible to an animus on the part of the critics against "public education." . . .

But by and large, the critics cherish the institution of public schooling, and they therefore seek to reform education within the framework of free education. . . . What is incredible is not that such charges are being made, but that they should be denied. The evidence is superabundant that there has been and is a strong collectivist leaning in many national teaching associations, in many textbooks, and hence in many classrooms throughout the country. . . .

There have been changes in the past fifteen years, of course. Some of the jagged edges of doctrinaire socialism have dulled. But the heart is still there, and there is incontrovertible evidence that an impressive number of teachers still hew to the collectivist line—in and out of class. . . .

The NEA [National Education Association] has entered into politics in the unvarnished sense: "My friends," reported Mr. Howard Dawson, Director of the Legislative Commission of the NEA, some years back, "we have recently had some demonstrations of the power of influence of teachers working in a righteous cause. It is no accident that Lister Hill returned to the Senate. . . . It was no political accident that Claude Pepper will again sit in the halls of the United States Senate. . . . Again, my friends, it is no political accident that that not-so-distinguished Republican Senator from Oregon, Mr. Holman, will not again grace the halls of Congress. . . ."

The teachers' organizations—and the teachers in general—have decided to stand up and be counted in various controversial issues. This is clearly their privilege, provided only that they recognize that the parent has a legitimate interest and a duty to inquire into the ideologies that are being promoted and inculcated in his child. He has a right to criticize a teacher, or a text, or a school.

It is this right which, in effect, the teaching associations and their publicists have refused to acknowledge. . . . We wonder just what role is left for us after the teachers' rights have been duly "protected."

THE AMERICAN LEGION POSITION [5]

Now, as never before in history, we find that people professing the same beliefs do not necessarily mean the same thing. . . . For too long now we have made objective truth subject to arbitrary opinion. In place of the fixed convictions on which the principles of democracy are founded, we have a sliding scale of values which permits varying interpretation. I am one of those who believe . . . that our teachers bear a primary responsibility for getting those principles back in their sockets.

There could be no better starting point than academic freedom itself. We are told by some that academic freedom entitles the educator to teach and preach as he pleases—that he functions in a kind of vacuum where no rules of conduct apply. Certainly that theory doesn't square with the principles of Washington and Jefferson and Lincoln.

One of the underlying questions of the moment is whether or not Communists should be permitted to teach in our schools and colleges. The mere fact of controversy on the matter re-

[5] From address by Lewis K. Gough, past commander of the American Legion, delivered before the 91st annual meeting of the National Education Association in Miami, July 3, 1953. *Congressional Record.* 99:A4721-2. July 18, 1953.

flects the general fuzziness of our thinking on fundamental values. We hold that the purpose of education is to present truths objectively and condition minds to seek these truths. And yet, the Communist party member is forbidden by the very nature of his belief from objective presentation of any subject.

Communists do not believe in academic freedom. They only use it, as they do all other freedoms in our society, to the end that they may destroy it. We teach law in our colleges but not by convicted criminals. Leprosy is explained, but not by lepers who might spread the infection. So communism should be taught but not by Communists—by qualified personnel who are capable of factual presentation.

The real threat of communism to America does not come from the so-called down-trodden classes. It comes from the men of eminence and distinction who have let themselves be used in the Communist cause. And I think it ought to be noted here that of this group, educators and scholars comprise by far the largest majority.

Let me cite an example. Of the sixty witnesses called before the House Committee on Un-American Activities during one year, only two were of foreign birth. The other fifty-eight, without exception, were native Americans of eminent learning— Phi Beta Kappas or Ph.D.'s or scholars of the first rank. Not one of the lot—and mark this, please—not one was a manual laborer or a farmer of the proletariat class which the Reds profess to speak for. And what kind of showing did these people make? Every one of them declined to answer questions posed by the Committee, on grounds of incriminating themselves.

These figures are not submitted for the purpose of questioning the collective loyalty of our teachers. The record of the great majority of our educators speaks for itself. But it would seem to me that those who make up that majority would feel compelled not only by national loyalty but by professional pride to vigorously repel the challenge to their good name.

Academic freedom is one thing, disloyalty quite another. When we countenance abuse of the one, we abet the other. If "academic freedom" is referred to as freedom of inquiry and research, then it is paramount to preserve that freedom if we are to enjoy our present way of life. If, however, academic freedom means the freedom to conspire against our Constitution and government, it becomes the concern of every citizen of the United States. Academic freedom does not include freedom from criticism and is not a shield to protect violation of the law. The American people look to the teachers and administrators of their schools for leadership in clarifying these doctrines and keeping the record straight.

What is important here—and what is generally not understood across the country—is that communism has made its deepest inroads in our educational ranks. Most of us have gone along assuming that labor has yielded the most ground. Meanwhile the quiet assault on our schools has been carried on with comparatively little notice. . . .

Academic freedom is threatened by many forces other than communism, but . . . the most immediate threat is the possibility that educators themselves will be unwilling to exclude Communists and Red-fronters from the shelter and immunity which academic freedom commands.

We must be careful not to become alarmists. We must be careful not to become Red-baiters in the negative sense. We must be doubly careful to keep clear in our own minds that concern for the rights of others without which democratic self-government dies. At the same time, we must not close our eyes to the proof of Communist infiltration into our American institutions.

AS THE RIGHT VIEWS THE LEFT [6]

The public-address system of the Left, from the educational columns of the New York *Times* to the ukases of the Civil Liberties Union, forever dins into our ears the unrealistic cliché that American colleges are dominated by conservatives. To those of us who know, this is a fantastic inversion of truth. In American colleges today the political and cultural Left is militant and

[6] From "Our Left-Handed Colleges," by E. Merrill Root, professor of English at Earlham College, Richmond, Indiana. *Freeman*. 3:50-2. October 20, 1952. Reprinted by permission.

ruthless—blatantly speaking, eagerly heard, while the political and cultural Right is ridiculed and patronized, and (to its own shame) inarticulate and passive. . . .

All the current blather broadcast by the academic bleeding-hearts, that radical and even liberal professors are "silenced" and "frightened" is camouflage for the infiltrating tanks of One Big Government. Who actually gets more space on the air, in the press, in textbooks, magazines, even twenty-five-cent books . . . than these Sons of the Left, from Schlesinger to Lattimore? Today the McLiberals are the fair-haired boys of the academic world, who can do no wrong and to whom no outraged parent may say scat. . . .

One is led to believe that every "liberal" professor in the country is a frightened, innocent little rabbit, panting his heart out in an academic bunny-hole. But does this truly describe . . . the almost unanimous furor against Buckley at Yale; the chorus of the pack from Pasadena to Poughkeepsie, giving tongue against any son (or daughter) of the Right?

The facts of academic life are vastly different from the alarums and excursions of the McLiberals. Long ago the former president of Earlham College, Dr. William Cullen Dennis, one of the wisest and most tolerant presidents I have known, made a remark which then seemed to me extreme, but which I have found increasingly true. He said that any radical professor in an American college, no matter how incompetent, had better chance of tenure than a conservative—for the president and the trustees are aware of the shrieks that will arise if he is dismissed. A conservative professor of like inability is certain to go. . . .

You can know the dominant teachers in American colleges by noting the *axioms of thinking* so deeply planted in students (and even in normally conservative professors) that they have become unconscious prejudices. Consider a few of these straws that indicate the secret wind of prejudice. Consider their prevalence, their unconscious habituality, and then ask if, like Topsy, they "just growed."

One omnipresent axiom in the consensus of academic thinking is that Senator McCarthy is an assassin of character, a political demon dealing in "smears" and "lies." At any academic
gathering you will find such castigation of the Senator implicit,
and if you linger long you will find it explicit. Yet I have
never heard in private or in public one word of academic criticism of the smears and lies of a Joliot-Curie or a Red Dean,
charging America with germ warfare in Korea. . . .

Again, the usual academic reaction to *Red Channels* is hostile.
It is considered "unfair" to colleges to list artists or teachers according to their own free choice of associates. Yet I have
never heard in colleges any private or public disgust at the un-
fairness of the *Nation* listing in its anniversary issue the evils
of America, with a few thrown in to make a baker's dozen.
Red Channels is "illiberal" to see straws moving in a single
direction and suggest a single wind; the *Nation* is "liberal" to
list an army of straw-men, and to charge that its ragged perversions prove America "close to fascism." This is the odd tendency
of the academic mind, whether of faculty or students, all over
the country. To notice what is wrong with Communists or
what is right with America is "illiberal"; to notice what is
right with Communists or what is wrong with America is "liberal." Why? . . .

If all this were a spirited half of a great debate, one might
say: "Truth will win." But it is as dictatorial as a column of
tanks moving up to occupy a country. The design of the Mc-
Liberals is to flatten out all opposition and to reduce the minds
of students and colleagues of the Right to inarticulate sub-
servience that must not make reply. . . . In the academic life,
you must believe all this phony bathos, or you are a "reactionary"
and one of the Republicans and sinners. Because you oppose
Red fascism, they call you a "Fascist." They whisper it, behind
your back, to your students, where it will hurt most. But this,
of course, is not "smearing," not "assassination of character."

Anyone who knows this college generation, knows that it
has somehow and somewhere been conditioned into such axioms
of error. Students believe (without knowing why or where

they learned it) that capitalism is "immoral" and socialism is "moral"; that America is always secretly "imperialistic," and Soviet Russia always (quite secretly) an emancipator. . . . They suppose that it is "liberal" to tolerate the intolerable, to acquiesce in the murder of liberty, to present your willing jugular to the stab of "the smiler with the knife" (how well Chaucer knew communism!). Who is to blame for the fact that they approach this crisis of history with the intellectual equipment of babes-in-the-wood?

Fundamentally the issue reduces itself to a question of values. All culture rests on certain premises, axioms, choices of the spirit: else there can be no action or thought. A people, at a great creative moment, through its greatest creative spirits, chooses certain values, qualities and meanings to give form and content to its life: these are its soul, its shaping dream, its Aristotelian "entelechy." . . . The great critics may and must clarify these, purge them of confusions and contradictions, develop them, even question details if they become idols that hold us back from God. But even the greatest critics must not destroy these values—only help to fulfill them. And most teachers are not, and should not seek to be, philosophers or critics— they have not the genius it requires. Teachers are conservers and transmitters of values, qualities and meanings. The people whom they serve have the right to say that the great values, qualities and meanings shall be conserved and transmitted by those who have been chosen because they are talented for, and should be dedicated to, such transmission. It is pretty to prate of the "academic freedom" of teachers to miseducate youth, but what of the freedom of parents to have their children taught the values by which they may live and not the perversions by which they will die?

The American dream has always insisted on the rights of the individual against the group, of the citizen against the state; of liberty to endure the least possible government. Teachers who reduce the individual to the hideous caricature known as "the Common Man," who slyly or blatantly uphold the encroachments of the total state, do not teach the values, qualities and meanings which parents wish taught. Parents have the right to say to such teachers: "If you wish to teach your own children these things, or if there are parents who wish you to teach such things and will support you while you do so, teach as you wish. But we are not going to support you with our taxes or our private tuition while you infect our children with the opposite of what we consider truth."

The pity is that parents are too humble and passive and do not say this often enough. They are awed by the spectacled Wise Men, the Pooh-Bahs of education. When they do revolt (as at Pasadena), the pundits of collectivism, being a reactionary, vested interest, lobby, gang up, and cry havoc. They must have the "freedom" to pursue their own profitable monopoly.

The collectivists and the nihilists have too long monopolized a revolutionary role—in order to bring about reaction. It is time for the many professors who have been gagged and trampled by the Left, for the parents who have been mocked and milked by the Left, for the students who have been hoodwinked and played for suckers by the Left, to rally against the Tories of collectivism, the Red Coats of socialism. Certainly if we fight the battle of freedom to the end, we can make the Tories capitulate.

FEDERAL INVESTIGATION OF EDUCATION

EDITOR'S INTRODUCTION

The present congressional inquiry into "subversive influence in the educational process" as it is termed by the Senate Judiciary subcommittee under Senator Jenner, or into "Communist methods of infiltration: education" as the House Committee on Un-American Activities under Congressman Velde puts it, is something new for Americans.

American education has traditionally been a local and a state concern. Federal aid to education has been bitterly opposed on the grounds that it would constitute "invasion" and possible domination of states' rights by the Federal Government. So when Congress announced in 1952 that it contemplated a large-scale inquiry into Communist influence in the schools, a sizable portion of the opposition to such inquiry came from conservative school administrators who felt that such investigation on the part of Federal authorities was improper. That feeling is still fairly widespread in many quarters and tends to obscure the basic issues involved in the question of what schools should do about Communist teachers or those suspected of being Communists.

The committees have generally ignored their critics, seemingly secure in the knowledge that they represent a fairly substantial body of public opinion, in view of the facts that congressional appropriations for both committees were increased substantially this year, and that no sizable opposition has developed within Congress itself. Indeed, Congressman Velde announced in April 1953 that the letters the House Un-American Activities Committee was receiving from educators were mostly favorable, and a spokesman for the American Council on Education expressed the opinion that "Mr. Velde has kept his activities within bounds."

But while organized educational groups refused to oppose the committees, individual educators did so, as did a number of leading churchmen and labor leaders. From Bishop G. Bromley Oxnam, a Methodist church leader, came this statement: "If there be a few subversives in the teaching staffs of this nation, there are proper agencies to deal with them." The National Council of the Churches of Christ in the United States of America issued a policy statement deploring investigations which would destroy confidence in American schools, and the threat to local control of the schools, saying, "The control of our educational institutions . . . is not a function of congressional committees, but is properly vested in boards of trustees . . . selected for that purpose." James B. Carey, of the CIO, doubted if schoolmen knew how to defend themselves "against a concerted attack animated by ignorance, reaction and bigotry."

Portions of the recent Jenner committee report are reproduced here to show the committee's avowed purpose, its method as well as its findings. The House Un-American Activities Committee follows generally the same procedure, and to a large extent its investigation has paralleled that of the Jenner committee. The major differences in the two committees seem to be in objectives. The Jenner committee seeks evidence of organized subversion, while the Velde committee is more concerned with individual educators.

SUBVERSION IN EDUCATION—JENNER COMMITTEE REPORT [1]

The Internal Security Subcommittee, in the second year of its inquiry into Communist penetration into the educational system, held hearings in Washington, New York, Boston, and Chicago. The subcommittee was continuing under Chairman William E. Jenner (Republican, Indiana) the inquiry into Communist penetration into the educational process begun in 1952 under the chairmanship of Senator Pat McCarran (Democrat, Nevada).

Altogether it heard more than a hundred witnesses in the field of education in public session and many more in executive

[1] From *Subversive Influence in the Educational Process*; report, July 17, 1953, of the subcommittee to investigate the administration of the Internal Security Act and other internal security laws, to the Senate Judiciary Committee. 83d Congress, 1st session. The Committee. Washington 25, D.C. 1953. p 1-14, 28-9.

session. Of this number eighty-two educators, about whom the subcommittee had evidence of Communist party membership, refused to answer questions about their Communist affiliations, invoking instead their constitutional privilege against self-incrimination. Three others admitted Communist party membership, but defied the committee in refusing to supply further details. Twenty were responsive witnesses.

Of the eighty-two, forty were faculty members or employees of sixteen different universities. The others were teachers in secondary schools or persons who held other positions in the educational system.

The subcommittee received evidence from former Communist organizers that the Soviet organization was continuously engaged in a plan to penetrate our educational institutions at every possible point, thus posing a serious threat to our national security. The Communist agents who spun the very real web of conspiracy and intrigue within the framework of the United States Government departments, in almost all cases, were cradled in our distinguished universities and colleges. The subcommittee observed that the universities and colleges are, understandably, more and more participating in government, creating policy and shaping our national destiny and that the expressions and sentiments of educators are more and more flowing into the mainstream of our national culture.

The subcommittee's function in the educational field is to examine the workings of the Communist apparatus and to determine whether it is necessary to have additional legislation against new and undefined crimes. The subcommittee has no authority or power to prosecute for criminal action. That is the function of the prosecuting arm of the executive branch of the Government. It is the function of the legislative branch of the Government to go forward and determine whether or not new laws are necessary or old laws are outmoded. . . .

At the beginning of this year, Senator Jenner issued for the subcommittee a statement of policy in which he said:

If a totalitarian organization such as the evidence shows to exist in our nation's schools is allowed to flourish in our institutions of learning unexposed and unchecked, not only will our youth be infused with seeds of their own and the nation's destruction, but academic freedom, the right to free inquiry, the right to dissent, the development of our culture, and the right to express free ideas and free thoughts will be choked and stifled.

Senator Jenner also said, during the course of the hearings: . . .

Our committee is not concerned with telling the leaders of our schools and colleges what to teach, or how to teach. It is concerned with showing them where this alien conspiracy is hidden. . . . It is concerned with helping our academic leaders to meet the threat. There can be no academic freedom until this Soviet conspiracy hidden in our schools and colleges is exposed to the light, and the rule of Moscow over its adherents in the educational world is broken.

Within this framework, the Internal Security Subcommittee . . . decided that its functions were:

(1) to expose secret members of the Communist network by its power to administer oaths and by it power of subpoena and its power to punish for contempt of Congress;

(2) to sketch the pattern of infiltration and subversion as it is outlined by the evidence;

(3) to make it possible for local educational authorities to observe effective measures taken by other localities and institutions;

(4) to help local agencies to strengthen the machinery available to them to identify Communists and remove existing obstacles to action; and

(5) to improve the Federal machinery for identifying Communists. . . .

In view of the fact that the subcommittee was working in a limited time range and without investigators, it could not examine all instances of local Communist activity in the field of education. It, therefore, selected as many instances as possible which contributed to a prevailing pattern.

The subcommittee, in viewing the whole scene at the outset, reaffirmed its recognition of the principle that exposure and elimination of subversion in education is primarily a responsibility of state, local, and private authorities. The subcommittee was called upon to act because of the almost complete inability of the educational authorities to expose the Communist conspiracy with the means available to them.

The chairman of the subcommittee stressed, from time to time, and the subcommittee followed this standard, that it would not interfere with the adminstration of educational institutions and would scrupulously refrain from passing judgment on the inaction of the local authorities in acting on the evidence produced by the subcommittee. Thus, the subcommittee maintained its principle of not interfering with the administration of educational institutions.

,The subcommittee sought as its determinant of subversion, membership in the Communist party and overt acts connected therewith. . . .

Recognizing that in the absence of an admission, only sworn testimony of someone who was formerly among the ranks of the Communist party can be evidence of another's Communist membership, the subcommittee took in executive session the testimony of responsible ex-Communists and reliable government agents. This testimony was not made public in any case until the persons so identified as Communists were given an opportunity in private session to contravert or deny the evidence. After these private sessions, the educators were then called before the subcommittee also in private session and asked about the details of the evidence, and their refusal to deny or contravert the evidence was followed by open hearings. The subcommittee felt that such a method was the most responsible procedure of exposing those who are Communists. Furthermore, it insured fairness and accuracy both to the witness and the subcommittee, since, according to this standard, the names of those who denied Communist party membership were not brought into the public record as subversives.

The subcommittee sought to make only present membership in the Communist party its norm of subversion. . . .

The subcommittee had noted the political phenomenon of particular educators rallying around and supporting Communist-controlled organizations that professed to espouse commendable causes but which were really fronts or covers for Communist purposes. The subcommittee noted with distress the extensive indulgence of educators in this activity and the harm such organizations wrought in sapping the national resistance. And yet because an individual's participation in such activity, however extensive, is ambiguous as evidence and may be consistent with gullibility and political confusion rather than actual subversion and membership in the Communist party, the subcommittee exposed such activity only after the individual could not contravert the subcommittee's evidence of his Communist party membership. . . .

Witnesses concerning whom the subcommittee had evidence of Communist membership, resorted with great frequency to claims that they had a right to refuse to testify because of the constitutional privileges granted by the Bill of Rights, which consists of the first ten amendments of the United States Constitution.

The two amendments most frequently referred to are the first and fifth. The First Amendment provides:

> Congress shall make no law respecting an establishment of religion, or prohibiting the free exercise thereof; or abridging the freedom of speech, or of the press; . . .

The Fifth Amendment provides:

> No person . . . shall be compelled in any criminal case to be a witness against himself. . . .

With respect to the First Amendment, the subcommittee determined that the court decisions have clearly held that a witness could not invoke his privilege under the First Amendment when asked about membership in the Communist party. This clear authority was largely a factor in causing the chairman, in every case, not to recognize invocation of that amendment as grounds for not answering. . . .

The subcommittee, however, did recognize the right of witnesses to claim privilege under the Fifth Amendment. In recognizing such claims, the subcommittee necessarily accepted the legal presumption that the witness, in each case, was invoking the privilege in good faith. On several occasions, the subcommittee expressed doubt about the actual good faith of the witness, yet invariably the committee allowed such claims. . . .

Moreover, the subcommittee could not fail to observe that in virtually every case the witness invoked his privilege against self-incrimination only when it became apparent that the evidence available to the subcommittee was so concrete and so substantial that a denial would expose him to possible prosecution; otherwise he unhesitatingly denied membership. . . .

For these reasons the subcommittee considered the claim of privilege, particularly on the question of Communist party membership, extremely significant in its determination of who are Communists.

The subcommittee has all along recognized the extreme difficulty of establishing the real facts of the Communist conspiracy. . . . The subcommittee experienced the same difficulty in determining the extent to which the Communists were able to penetrate the educational process of the nation.

Only someone who has been behind the closed doors of the conspiracy is competent to testify as to the number and identity of persons who participate in the conspiracy. So again the best evidence on the extent of the infiltration was the testimony of responsible ex-Communists and reliable government agents. The length of time involved for a Communist to make a complete break with the organization and its ideology and to acquire the outlook necessary to testify to the details of his participation in the Communist party was such that it was impossible to determine from ex-Communists the present status of infiltration. . . .

Bella V. Dodd, for instance, broke with the Communist party in 1948. She testified that it was not until 1952 that she became sufficiently disentangled, emotionally, from her Communist ties to see her way clear to testify before a Senate committee. But by that time her competency to testify to direct events after 1948 had vanished, because she no longer had access to Communist secrets after her defection. . . .

Dr. Dodd had been legislative representative of the New York Teachers' Union and later a member of the national committee of the Communist party. Testimony, such as hers, despite its limitation of time and perspective, is unusual, and the subcommittee was indeed fortunate in getting a glimpse through that source behind the curtain of the Communist conspiracy.

Dr. Dodd testified that the New York Teachers' Union, of which she was a leader, achieved a membership of 11,000 teachers, of which 1,000 were members of the Communist party.

She further testified that the union had considerably more Communists than was necessary to control that organization, so extensive was the influence of the controlling Communists. Some of these were used in building other Communist organizations. Dr. Dodd testified that nationally, up to 1948, the peak of the Communist strength among educators was about 1,500 members. She said on this score . . . , "The East had the large proportion. There were some in Chicago and a small block out in the California area, but the East was the place where you had the large number." . . .

John Lautner, who had been an organizer for the Communist party as late as January 1950 . . . testified that in 1949 and early 1950 he was given the assignment by his Communist superiors of forming a secret network in New York State. About five hundred of the Communist teachers in New York were assigned to him for the purpose of being processed into the underground. . . .

One witness testified that in the early 1940's there were thirty to forty members in a faculty branch of the Communist party at City College in New York. In addition he had attended several meetings of a New York City-wide unit of college professors and instructors that contained more than a hundred Communist members from all colleges in New York City. Another testified to the size of the Brooklyn College unit of the party. Two contemptuous witnesses acknowledged that they belonged to a unit at Columbia made up of almost a dozen faculty members and units at Pennsylvania and Yale made up of a dozen faculty members and students respectively. Bella Dodd gave a list of colleges that contained to her knowledge Communist cells of one or more faculty members. And finally, there were the eighty-two educators from sixteen universities and various other educational institutions and services selectively subpoenaed by the subcommittee to give a concrete sketch of successful Communist penetration.

Moreover, Mrs. Rose Russell, the present legislative representative of the New York Teachers' Union, estimated that at the time of her testimony, September 23, 1952, the union membership was "over 4,000" persons. It was apparent to the subcommittee that that number of teachers, therefore, remained organizationally under Communist control in New York City, but it could not fail to conclude that legislative inquiries had been effective in reducing the union's sphere of influence from 11,000 members, the high point, according to Dr. Dodd, to the figure given by Mrs. Russell. The subcommittee could not learn how many of these 4,000 were actually members of the Communist party.

William Jansen, superintendent of schools for New York City, said that a program instituted by the Board of Education in New York to eliminate Communist teachers, had, with the help of congressional committees, caused 81 teachers to be separated from the school system as of the date of his testimony, March 25, 1953, when 180 others were still under investigation.

Richard E. Combs, chief counsel for the California Senate Committee on Un-American Activities, testified to the work being performed by the California state legislative body in dealing with the problem of Communist infiltration of the state's educational institutions. Mr. Combs told the subcommittee how the college presidents of all major California colleges cooperated with the state senate committee there, and together caused the removal of more than a hundred faculty members from those universities between June 24, 1952, and the date of this testimony on March 24, 1953. On this score and on the score of preventing still other Communists from being retained, Mr. Combs said:

MR. MORRIS [committee counsel]: Have you had any results since that time, since you have had this general alliance?

MR. COMBS: About one hundred faculty members have been removed from the faculties as a result of this plan since the 24th of last June.

MR. MORRIS: So your testimony, Mr. Combs, is that since last June—June 1952—because of the cooperative effort on the part of your committee and the various college presidents and their staffs, more than one hundred members of California faculties have been removed from their teaching jobs?

MR. COMBS. That is correct. In addition to that, Mr. Morris, the committee deemed it expedient to indicate to the university administrators the necessity, particularly in the larger institutions, of employing full-time people who had had a practical experience in the field of counter-Communist activities, ex-FBI agents, and ex-Navy and military intelligence men. That has been followed.

On the major colleges and campuses in California such persons are working and have been for almost since last June. They maintain a liaison with our committee. We in turn make available to them the accumulated documentation, the material that we have accumulated during the [last] fourteen years. But we soon found that it was even more necessary to prevent people from getting on faculties and obtaining positions in the educational institutions than it was to get rid of them once their positions became solidified.

So the committee devoloped a procedure whereby applicants for positions are referred to us, their names are, and if we do have any documentation concerning their Communist activity over a long period of time we make that available to the university as a guide to indicate whether or not the individual should be employed.

MR. MORRIS: Mr. Combs, is it your testimony that in addition to the work of exposing Communists on the various faculties that you also aid the California colleges in keeping off the faculty in the first place people who are either Communists or about whom there is evidence concerning Communist activity?

MR. COMBS: Yes, sir; we feel that that is fully as important as getting them out of faculties once they get entrenched.

Because of the testimony of Mr. Combs the subcommittee, feeling that the exposure was being accomplished by local agencies, did not subpoena any witnesses from California. This was the standard the subcommittee had set for itself on leaving to local authorities wherever possible the job of exposing subversion.

The subcommittee sought to conduct its hearings in such a way as to encourage wherever possible local awareness of and resistance to Communist infiltration.

In the first place, it had no investigators in the field. There was enough evidence of subversion discernible to the subcommittee and its staff, to obviate the need of investigators. But it could not fail to observe that the available evidence so accessible was most plentiful where there had been a prior state or local investigation. In New York City, the New York State Legislature, under the chairmanship of then State Senator Frederic R. Coudert, Jr., had conducted an inquiry in 1940 and 1941 into subversion in the New York City schools and colleges. This state subcommittee had made impressive inroads into the Communist network in New York. Bella Dodd, a leader of the Communist organization which was investigated at the time, acknowledged this very readily.

However, that investigation was discontinued in 1941 when the Soviet Union entered the war, and thereafter the political atmosphere became favorable once again to Communist expansion.

The Internal Security Subcommittee reopened the inquiry. It called fifteen teachers from the secondary schools and fourteen from the city colleges, many of whom had been called eleven years before in the Rapp-Coudert inquiry but had, at that time, denied any Communist affiliation. After refusing to answer similar questions at the congressional hearings, all these educators were suspended or dismissed by the New York City authorities under the provision of the city charter which prohibits city employees from refusing to testify. . . .

Most of the fourteen New York City college teachers who were subpoenaed by this subcommittee during the present hearings and who invoked their constitutional protection were subjects of the Rapp-Coudert committee investigation in 1941. However, because most of these and others who comported themselves in similar fashion in executive session before this subcommittee, denied Communist party membership in 1941 . . . they were able to stay on unmolested for twelve years teaching thousands of students in their characteristic way. . . .

Dr. Gideonse [president of Brooklyn College] testified fully how he possessed knowledge through these twelve years that some members of his faculty were Communists, and yet he was powerless to do anything about it until these teachers invoked their privilege before this subcommittee. This was so because he had neither the legal nor the investigation power to go beyond the evidence made available in the Rapp-Coudert investigation. . . .

In all but a few of the cases before the subcommittee, the university officials and local authorities suspended the teachers who invoked their privilege against incrimination when asked about Communist party membership. The following universities suspended faculty members therefor: Rutgers, Brooklyn Polytechnic Institute, Columbia, Vermont, New York University, Queens, Hunter, City College of New York and Brooklyn. . . .

From all the evidence taken to date, the subcommittee has come to these conclusions:

1. World Communist leaders have made schools and colleges of the United States a target of infiltration and activity as part of their program to destroy the United States.

2. A Communist educator, because of his submission to a totalitarian organization, cannot maintain the standards of academic freedom and objective scholarship and be loyal to the regulations of local authorities.

3. Communist teachers use their positions in the classroom and in extra-curricular activities to subvert students and other teachers and the public to promote the objectives of communism.

4. Communist teachers exercise as part of an organized conspiracy an influence far more extensive than their numbers would indicate.

5. Communist penetration of the schools is becoming more covert, and Communist teachers are being organized into a secret underground more difficult to detect.

6. Teachers, students, and educational authorities, public and private, do not today have the means to identify, unassisted, secret members of the Communist party or to trace their conspiratorial activities.

7. Exposure of Communists by congressional and state legislative committees has helped local authorities protect themselves against organized subversion and has given such authorities the evidence by which some hidden Communists could be removed from teaching positions.

8. Since the great majority of present-day secret Communists can, only with great difficulty, be identified by evidence sufficient to justify legal action, it falls upon the educators themselves to devise criteria and methods to deal with teachers whose adherence to the Communist conspiracy, though not easily legally provable, makes them morally unfit to teach as well as a threat to national security.

9. A teacher who invokes his privilege against incrimination rather than deny membership in the Communist organization before a duly constituted authority, violates his trust and forfeits his right to shape the character of our youth.

The subcommittee makes the following recommendations:

That educational authorities give consideration to the establishment of criteria and the initiation of procedures whereby schools, colleges and universities can eliminate teachers who have demonstrated their unsuitability to teach, because of their collaboration with the Communist conspiracy.

That states and educational institutions give consideration to the program adopted by the state of California, and the several colleges and universities therein, which, recognizing that subversion in the educational process is a matter of public concern, has put into operation a program that provides for a reservoir of security information, the free exchange of security information between colleges and legislative committees, and means whereby the facilities and powers of state agencies are made of service to educational institutions.

That school authorities, colleges, and local boards of education institute positive programs, under qualified experts in the field of combating communism, to teach both teachers and school pupils the nature of the Communist conspiracy that is attacking the whole structure of our society.

A VOTE IN FAVOR OF CONGRESSIONAL INVESTIGATIONS [2]

As one who taught in a series of educational institutions in the United States for some twenty-one years, my attitude is that the schools of the United States should welcome at all times

[2] From remarks on the floor of the Senate by Senator Wayne Morse (Independent, Oregon). *Congressional Record.* 99:1378. February 20, 1953.

any investigation any congressional committee, acting within its powers of investigation, decides to conduct.

I believe that the educators who seek to use pressures to arouse public opinion against the exercise of the power of investigation make a great mistake. Of course, they place themselves in an illogical position when they take the position that because they do not like Committee X or Committee Y or Chairman A or Chairman B of those committees, therefore liberals should try to prevent investigations of education and of educational institutions. If they should prevent such investigations, in my judgment they would be guilty of violating one of the basic principles of true liberalism, which is to maintain in effective operation the system of checks and balance which in these days is so little understood . . . by the American people. . . .

One great principle is that public institutions should at all times be subjected to public surveillance and evaluation regarding how they are carrying out their public functions. The trust and the obligation which rest upon the schools of the United States are solemn ones, and from the standpoint of the rights of individuals, they are also almost sacred ones.

Therefore, I believe the response of the educators of America should be, "Welcome, welcome; come forward with your investigation." The schools of the United States have a great opportunity if they will only recognize it, to educate the American people on the question of academic freedom and in the search for the truth, no matter where it leads, for, after all, to inculcate truth is the greatest obligation of the school system of the United States.

AN EDITORIAL OPINION [3]

One need not enter a defense for all the methods of the House and Senate committees investigating communism to feel amazement and disgust at the parade of smart aleck professors who have been appearing before them and thumbing unscholarly noses at their country.

Men who love their country do not behave that way. Most of us are loyal to our nation, even though we may disagree

[3] From "They're Not Bigger than the United States," editorial. Philadelphia *Inquirer*. p 14. March 22, 1953. Reprinted by permission.

sharply with things done by certain public officials. But when we see supposed educators . . . not only defying the committee but trying to make a travesty of its whole proceedings—we can only cheer when such men are promptly given the heave-ho by universities they so shamefully misrepresent. . . .

We should never forget that the Red fifth column in America, and all the fellow travelers who do its bidding and sign its petitions, are quite as much a part of the Soviet war machine as the soldiers who shoot down our GI's in Korea.

It is against this frame of reference that we should consider the present investigation, and the procession of professors, some of whom are not Communists, but many of whom seem to think they are bigger than their country and owe no loyalty to it.

As editors, we would be the last in the world to help curb any expression of opinion, any right of dissent, or any freedom to champion unpopular causes. But the Soviet conspiracy to infiltrate government, schools, and labor unions is not dissent, and those who serve that conspiracy are not exercising civil liberties, but helping to destroy civil liberties. . . .

We do not presume to sit in judgment on all the witnesses who have been appearing in Washington. But we do believe that men who are really devoted to their country usually lean over backward to avoid appearing to aid its enemies. Indeed, the vast majority of educators wisely set an example of citizenship, loyalty, and ordinary good manners, show respect for the institutions of the United States, and are not too intellectual to conceal the fact that they love a nation which has given us all more freedom than ever has been possessed by any other people on earth.

To those who oppose the methods of Senator McCarthy, Representative Velde and others, we suggest the answer is not to champion Communists or to cheer professorial bumpkins too big for their boots. The answer is to take the initiative in cleaning the remaining Reds out of our institutions; to render them harmless by stripping from them the respectable masks of liberalism, academic freedom, and civil rights behind which they have been hiding and doing the Kremlin's dirty work.

A PLEA FOR LOCAL CONTROL [4]

The existence of the Communist conspiracy in our own midst has stirred deep and natural anxieties—anxieties which are being exploited by unscrupulous politicians. And, at the same time, the existence of this conspiracy has raised hard and urgent questions not easily answered by the familiar formulas of civil freedom.

One of these questions is: Where does the Communist teacher fit into the scheme of academic freedom? The only reasonable answer is: He does not. . . .

Fortunately, according to all available exidence, the actual number of Communist teachers in American colleges is exceedingly small. Recently, however, there has been a tendency for abrogations of academic freedom to be committed under the disingenuous excuse of "protecting the colleges against communism."

There are, unfortunately, many people whose horror of communism is matched only by their horror of the free and critical intellect. It is therefore incumbent upon all those who are genuinely concerned with meeting the Communist danger to proceed with the utmost scrupulousness and to be quick to admit that a teacher's opinions are no concern of the state so long as he reaches them in the course of honest inquiry.

However, after this has been said, there remains the question of what to do about the Communist teachers who do exist. We see no reason why this matter cannot be left in the hands of the colleges, and their faculties, themselves. Because there is almost universal agreement that membership in the Communist party is a professional disqualification for the academic life, it does not follow necessarily that there need be a strict uniformity in the implementation of this belief. . . .

Because the number of actual Communist teachers is so minute, because even when augmented by the number of "fellow-travelers" they are still a tiny fraction of the college teaching profession, there is no justification for a congressional committee to

[4] From "Freedom to Teach," letter to the editor, by George S. Counts, Paul R. Hays, Sidney Hook, and Arthur O. Lovejoy, members, Commission on Academic Freedom, American Committee for Cultural Freedom. New York *Times*. p E 10. July 19, 1953. Reprinted by permission.

concern itself with the problem. There is no national problem—there is not even anything that can be described as a state-wide problem—and there is no imaginable legislation that can flow from the congressional inquiries now under way. The only net effect they can have is to demoralize the teaching profession by making it feel that it works under a perpetual cloud of suspicion and distrust.

The autonomy of the university, its relative freedom from outside pressures and external constraints, is a prize hard won by centuries of effort, and only the most extreme circumstances can excuse any encroachment upon it. There are no such extreme circumstances in this country today.

CONGRESSIONAL INVESTIGATIONS— AAUP STAND [5]

The Thirty-ninth Annual Meeting of the American Association of University Professors reaffirms the protest of the Thirty-eighth Annual Meeting of the Association against the tendency, in legislative investigations relating to loyalty, toward using the professional writings and utterances, and the lawful personal associations of individuals, to impugn their loyalty without regard to context of time or circumstances. This meeting does not question the power of Congress to conduct investigations for the purpose of securing factual information as a basis for legislation, but reaffirms and reasserts the basic principle of American constitutional law that the function of the legislative branch of the Government is the enactment of legislation and not the prosecution of individuals. . . . The proper efforts of the government to protect itself against subversion, as against any other harmful acts, are limited to the enactment of legislation defining and proscribing specific acts as subversive and to the prosecution of individuals who commit legally defined subversive acts, including conspiracy to commit such acts. These efforts should not include the penalizing of thought, expressions of opinion, or personal relationships.

[5] From resolution adopted by the American Association of University Professors [AAUP] at its 39th Annual Meeting in Chicago, March 27-28, 1953. *American Association of University Professors Bulletin.* 39:93-4. Spring 1953. Reprinted by permission. (Passages of the statement dealing with other aspects of academic freedom are reprinted on p 119-20 and p 138-9 of this book.)

Legislative investigations which are in fact trials of individuals, based on thoughts and opinions, or on personal relationships, encroach upon and discourage freedom of thought, of inquiry, and of expression. Such investigations are, therefore, contrary to basic principles of our constitutional system and inimical to the welfare of the nation.

A ROUNDUP OF MIDWEST OPINION [6]

Congressional investigations are dim possibilities to most mid-American colleges, but many of them are concerned that freedom of inquiry should not be restricted by the current atmosphere. . . .

Away from the large cities, for the most part, established in rural and racially homogeneous communities, most mid-American colleges have little cause to fear any possible Communist influence. Racial and economic tensions in the big cities of America have bred what communism there is, and the causes do not seem to exist in the rural mid-continent.

Reports from the campuses of mid-America follow:

ARKANSAS

There has never been any action on the state level to investigate the colleges for subversive activities, and there has been little consideration of the congressional probe of colleges. People . . . seem scarcely to realize it is going on. . . .

INDIANA

A 1951 legislative act rewritten in the attorney general's office for constitutionality would have set up a state commission to probe Communist activities. For some reason the section numbers were left out, and the law became inoperative. . . .

No law came out of the 1953 legislature pertaining to investigation of college professors or others regarding Communist affiliations.

[6] From "Schools in Midwest Defend Freedom of Inquiry—Even into Communism," news story. *Christian Science Monitor.* p4. June 15, 1953. Reprinted by permission.

IOWA

Iowa is probably typical of much of the Midwest—little feeling on the part of educators that there is a real Communist threat. However, one recent development shows that the current atmosphere of uncertainty does reach here.

Some time ago at Iowa State College a division of the faculty was reported over whether the writings of Karl Marx, principal Communist philosopher, should be used as required reading in a course in humanities.

Teachers involved in the course voted against including the "Communist Manifesto" by Marx and Frederick Engels on the required reading lists, according to the Associated Press. . . .

KENTUCKY

In six Kentucky schools—the University of Kentucky, the University of Louisville, Eastern, Berea, Centre, and Kentucky State Colleges—there seems to be a lack of widespread fear of a congressional investigation.

Nor has any faculty member interviewed indicated that free expression by him of honest thought and opinion might lead to the loss of his job. Chief fear seemed to be that of social disapproval and the "left-winger" tag. . . .

There apparently have arisen no clear issues involving academic freedom in Kentucky schools. Several educators said this is because Kentucky has, on the whole, a conservative tradition, a tradition decidedly inhospitable to radical thinking or teaching. So called left-wingers just aren't attracted to Kentucky schools.

Dr. William F. O'Donnell, president of Eastern Kentucky State College, put it this way:

"The South is probably less affected by 'isms' than any other part of the country. That makes it one of the best sources of teacher supply. The issue of academic freedom has never arisen here; we just take it for granted." . . .

LOUISIANA

At Tulane, as a typical large school in Louisiana, the attitude is that communism is not a problem. The president, Rufus Carrolton Harris, has made it plain that Tulane would never appoint Communists to its faculty and that "the greatest precautions are observed." . . .

MICHIGAN

Full cooperation with any proposed congressional investigation committee was promised by spokesmen for the University of Michigan and Wayne University.

But educators in general, including leaders in teaching groups, left no doubt that the rights of the individual would be protected should any of their number be called as a witness before the committee.

Dr. Harlan H. Hatcher, president of the University of Michigan, made clear the position of his institution in a telegram January 9, addressed to Representative Harold H. Velde [Republican] of Illinois.

In it, he promised full cooperation with the committee investigating Red influences in the nation's educational system, but reiterated that "the university has exercised all vigilance consistent with American practice against the possibility of subversive activities."

In the event that the university and its personnel come directly under investigation, a university spokesman said, . . . the university administration would advise that the persons go willingly and answer questions as asked. . . .

MISSOURI

Missouri reports "no fuss at all about prospective college investigations. There is little suspicion directed against Missouri schools generally, and administrators and faculties are planning no special action.

However, there has been considerable concern over possible damage that investigations might do to academic communities generally. Arthur H. Compton, chancellor of Washington University in St. Louis, said recently that "the safety of our nation and the healthy growth of our free society depend upon our having competent scholars who inquire searchingly into every problem that concerns us and tell us freely what they find. . . ."

He expressed misgivings at the policy of congressional investigation and asked if the public could expect a reliable judgment from "men alert to political advantage."

Thomas A. Spragens, president of Stephens College, said he believes there is little active communism in American education: "Although there is reason to be concerned about subversive influences in education, we face the danger that those who do not understand the basic philosophies of American education may threaten these freedoms in their overzealousness."

NEBRASKA

The feeling in Nebraska is that it is quite remote from congressional investigations. The report from the University of Nebraska is that it is not at all alarmed over any possible probes —at least one from any national source.

The one exception stems from State Senator Terry Carpenter, who remarked recently in the legislature that he was "going to ask Senator McCarthy to investigate the state university." This remark came just as the university's budget was coming up for consideration.

This came after Joseph J. Vinardi, head of the state's American Legion's Un-American Activities Committee, said that "a certain book was urged by a certain professor at the University of Nebraska . . . that some students had objected to the book . . . and that the post might look into it."

This book was *State of Asia*, a compilation containing a chapter by Owen J. Lattimore and one by Lawrence Rosinger, who, when questioned by the McCarran committee, claimed protection of the Fifth Amendment to avoid a question concerning possible Communist affiliations. The "certain professor" turned out to be a highly respected and completely unsuspect man.

This episode caused a statement of principles concerning academic freedom to be issued by the local chapter of the American Association of University Professors [AAUP]. Also, the executive committee of the Nebraska department of the American Legion thanked "the members of the teaching profession and their organizations for the great assistance rendered to the

Americanism program of the American Legion" and commended the school boards and other administrators for their "careful selection of teachers, faculties and administrators who are loyal to American premises of liberty."

This Legion committee also reaffirmed its faith in academic freedom and praised those schools "which are doing their best, by realistic American teaching, to reveal the truth about communism, socialism, fascism, and other undemocratic systems."

OKLAHOMA

As far as Tulsa University is concerned, it considers any problem of communism remote and it has never had such a problem.

At the University of Oklahoma, a school with a more complex and larger faculty, there is the same feeling. The president, George Cross, says that "no plans have been made here because of our belief that there is extreme unlikelihood of Oklahoma's being checked."

SOUTH DAKOTA

Congressional investigation into college administrations has stirred only mild interest hereabouts.

At South Dakota College, for instance, the president, John W. Headley, declares that if any faculty member were to start teaching subversive doctrine in his institution, it would be known on the campus almost at once. . . .

WISCONSIN

The congressional investigation storm hasn't hit Wisconsin yet. Some educators here, however, are indicating concern.

AAUP chapters at the Wisconsin State College, a tax-supported institution; Marquette University, a Roman Catholic institution; and the University of Wisconsin at Madison have so far done nothing to combat the threat.

The administrations of the three institutions, likewise, have not come forth with plans or statements to keep the congressional investigations in perspective.

An official at the Wisconsin State College said that AAUP membership is growing in Wisconsin. He said he believed it is growing because faculty members realize that the AAUP will fight for their rights. . . .

Perhaps the most significant development occurred in Madison recently, when 120 persons, some of them faculty members at the University of Wisconsin, met at the Loraine Hotel to form a Wisconsin chapter of the American Civil Liberties Union. . . .

When Abner Berry, Negro affairs editor of the New York *Daily Worker*, spoke at the University of Wisconsin last January 14, legislators became aroused. Mr. Berry spoke under the sponsorship of the university chapter of the Labor Youth League, a Marxist group on the attorney general's subversive list.

About three hundred students laughed, jeered, and heckled Mr. Berry during a question and answer period.

DANGERS OF "WELCOMING" INVESTIGATIONS [7]

I think that many university professors and presidents are failing to recognize the real peril presented—to themselves and to the society they serve—by the current congressional investigations of their institutions.

There seems to be a widespread tendency to treat these investigations as minor irritations to be borne philosophically or as bridges to be crossed when reached with a little caution and circumspection. Not very long ago, for example, the Association of American Colleges adopted a resolution in which it expressly declared that "the colleges should welcome any free and impartial inquiry" as a means of promoting popular understanding of the accomplishments of higher education.

A panel of the American Council on Education met fairly recently in Washington and split sharply, according to press reports, as to whether to welcome or deplore the congressional investigations of colleges and universities. A minority called upon educators to join in protest against the investigations as a threat

[7] From "Universities and Political Authority," by Alan Barth, member of the editorial staff of the Washington *Post* and author of *The Loyalty of Free Men*. *American Association of University Professors Bulletin*. 39:5-15. Spring 1953. Reprinted by permission.

to academic freedom. A majority, holding that there was nothing to fear from such inquiries, contended that educators could not claim "freedom of thought" for themselves while denying "freedom of investigation" to Congress.

And finally, the chairman of this panel, President Lewis W. Jones of Rutgers University, declared just lately, in a statement designed to justify his dismissal of two faculty members for declining to cooperate with just such a congressional investigation, that "public investigation of the universities is legitimate, and should be frankly met. It implies no invasion of academic independence." . . .

I am convinced that the attitude of hospitality and welcome toward congressional investigations is a mistaken one, both in terms of expediency and in terms of principle. So far as expediency is concerned, it pitches the inevitable battle on the worst possible ground from the universities' point of view; and so far as principle is concerned, it gives away the essential moral basis of resistance to what is, really, a barbarian invasion of American intellectual life. . . .

A congressional hearing . . . is a disadvantageous ground on which to fight the battle for academic freedom. It provides, to begin with, an atmosphere entirely unfriendly and unfamiliar to men of learning . . . an atmosphere in which the presentation of a considered and reasoned argument is virtually impossible. . . .

The notion that under such auspices it will be feasible to promote public understanding of what universities are doing and why they need academic freedom to fulfill their vital function seems to me completely naïve. . . . It is perfectly clear that the discussion in such a hearing is not going to be about academic freedom. . . . It will be a discussion not of principles but of personalities.

Thus these hearings will revolve around such questions as whether Professor A is a Communist because Louis Budenz says that someone told him that Professor A was believed to be a Communist a quarter of a century ago. It will revolve around such questions as whether Professor B is subversive because he belongs or once belonged to organizations which have incurred the disapproval of the Attorney General or the House Committee on Un-American Activities. It will revolve around such questions as whether a particular college is Communist-dominated because it allowed on its campus a visiting lecturer who denounced the Un-American Activities Committee. It will revolve around such questions as whether a university is Red because Allen Zoll doesn't like its textbooks or some of its teachers.

Out of this kind of inquiry and discussion can come only divisive controversy and confusion. . . . The committee, presumably, will be able to discover a few present members of the Communist party on college campuses. They will doubtless also be able to discover a number of teachers who joined the party years ago for respectable reasons, who got out of it years ago for respectable reasons, and who do not now choose—for equally respectable reasons—to make witnessing a career. . . .

Not long ago, Rutgers University dismissed two members of its faculty because they had invoked the protection of the Fifth Amendment in refusing to answer questions before the Senate Internal Security Subcommittee. Lesser institutions have cooperated with this committee or with the House Committee on Un-American Activities in the same way. Indeed, the latter was able to announce proudly not long ago that of thirty-nine university professors who had availed themselves of their constitutional privilege against self-incrimination thirty-seven had already been dismissed by their institutions.

For my own part, I think that teachers who plead this privilege are neither admirable nor astute. But if they are to be automatically disciplined for doing so, the committee will have developed a formidable method for determining the membership of university faculties—something which ought to be determined by the faculties themselves in a free society. . . .

Universities, and the individual members of the faculties, have, of course, a duty of respectful cooperation with any duly constituted congressional body. But this duty does not require of them blind obedience. They have a duty also to their own values which obliges them to judge each case individually on its individual merits. . . .

A college "welcome" for these investigations . . . is mistaken because it does violence to the fundamental principle that institutions of higher learning ought to be independent of the government in the same way, and for much the same reasons, that the church and the press are independent of the government. They cannot make their vital contribution to a free society if they are subject to political control. . . .

I am not questioning the legal authority of Congress to investigate institutions of higher learning . . . the church or the press. . . . Congress has plenary power . . . to look into any area of American life. But to say that Congress has power to investigate is not necessarily to say that this power ought to be exercised. In my own view, it ought resolutely to be eschewed in regard to universities . . . [since] their business is to produce men and women who will question inherited values and challenge constituted authority. . . .

The notion that religion, the press, and the universities should serve the state is essentially a Communist notion. Government control of these institutions is a distinguishing characteristic of every totalitarian system.

The administration of state universities has generally been delegated to boards of regents, responsible ultimately to state legislatures but never to the Federal Government. . . . And these have been, on the whole, sober, conscientious, and capable governing bodies—in no need whatever of congressional supervision. Generally speaking, these boards can be confidently relied upon for patriotism and sound judgment. For my own part, as a loyal Yale alumnus, I had rather by a good deal see my alma mater governed by Robert A. Taft in his capacity as a member of the Yale Corporation than by Robert A. Taft in his capacity as a member of the United States Senate. In the former capacity, it seems to me, he is much less likely to be swayed by partisan or other political considerations.

If American universities . . . "welcome" congressional investigation today, they will end by embracing congressional control tomorrow. If they let a congressional committee purge professors now, they will eventually let it control curricula. The seeds of ultimate surrender are sown inexorably in seemingly trivial and innocent concessions.

EFFECT ON THE COLLEGES [8]

The big question on United States educators' minds: What over-all effect are the investigations having on the nation's colleges and universities?

Most top educators seemed to agree that (1) Congress has a right to investigate whatever it pleases, and (2) Communists should be barred from teaching. Nor was anyone in a state of panic. And yet, the climate of the campuses had already begun to change. The investigations, said Dean Milton Muelder of Michigan State College, "have cast a pall, a shadow, creating doubt as to how far scholars can now go in discussing controversial issues."

If it were not for the personalities and methods of the investigators themselves—Velde, Jenner and McCarthy—the shadow might not loom so large. But the nation's teachers feel they have little reason to trust their accusers, and their attitudes towards the investigators range from resentment to contempt. "For the most part," says Harvard's Mark DeWolfe Howe, "a committee ascertains in a closed hearing the facts it needs to know. Following that, it proceeds to conduct an open meeting, with the realization that the people who kept silent will keep silent and suffer public disgrace." They are, adds President Philip Davidson of the University of Louisville, "unnecessary, irresponsible fishing expeditions" that could well destroy public confidence in the whole teaching profession.

Apparently they are beginning to destroy the profession's confidence in itself. For students and teachers alike, the new watchword seems to have become "caution," and, says President Virgil Hancher of the State University of Iowa, "Teachers were never meant to be cautious." . . . The academic motto for 1953 is fast becoming: "Don't say, don't write, don't go."

[8] From "The Danger Signals," news story. *Time.* 61:85-8. April 13, 1953. Reprinted by special permission of the editors. Copyright 1953. Time Inc.

THE STATES AND SUBVERSION

EDITOR'S INTRODUCTION

The Federal Government has had at least one Un-American Activities Committee functioning since 1940, and although schools and colleges were not previously considered targets for investigation by Federal authorities, the old Dies Committee of the House of Representatives (and its successors) preached the dangers of Communist infiltration from its inception. State activities, on the other hand, have taken a somewhat different approach. For one thing, only four states have had widely-publicized or especially active legislative committees investigating subversive activities in the schools. These four—the Rapp-Coudert Committee in New York (1940-1941); the Canwell Committee in Washington (1947-1948); the Tenney Committee in California (in one form or another from 1940 to the present time, but especially 1941-1949); and the Broyles Committee in Illinois (1947-1950)—stirred public opinion, and in three instances achieved the firing of a number of suspected Communists, as well as alarming educators of both liberal and conservative persuasion throughout America. There have been other state investigating committees, but their efforts were less publicized, generally without the repercussions in academic circles which characterized the activities of these four.

Several states have passed highly significant pieces of legislation affecting the schools and colleges. Most state legislation has dealt with public school teachers, in their capacity as public employees, and only incidentally with college teachers. But in those instances where state investigating committees have been established, the colleges have been a primary target. Resulting requests for legislation have often been directed specifically to colleges and universities. However, state control of public instruction differs so markedly from state to state that the measures adopted have shown very little similarity.

Since in most state legislation, public school teachers, as well as teachers in colleges and universities, are lumped together under the law, it is necessary to review pertinent legislation of a more general character. Further, because it is impossible to extract only those provisions dealing with the higher educational institutions, this section will deal briefly with some of the laws which relate chiefly to public school teachers who are under direct control by the state. The same laws affect teachers in the colleges and universities of the state less directly.

Discussion of California's loyalty oath law, which brought the whole subject of teachers' oaths into the limelight, is reserved for more detailed consideration in the next section.

Neither space nor time permits a complete résumé of all activities and laws in the several states which have touched upon the problem of freedom and loyalty in the colleges. Many non-legislative episodes have occurred: pressure groups have sought the removal of unpopular teachers; veterans' organizations and individuals have taken upon themselves, on occasion, to act as screening committees or community censors of speakers, textbooks, and teachers. But these unofficial actions have been relatively few in number—fairly isolated instances, with little organized support. For the purposes of this discussion they can be dismissed as of little importance to the broader issues at hand.

BASIS FOR STATE LEGISLATION [1]

When the American state legislatures had adjourned their 1950 sessions, they left behind them statute books containing well over three hundred enactments, aimed at what may be lumped together as subversive activities. . . . One hesitates to define a term that the states themselves use without precision. Subversion, say the legislatures is to be stifled or investigated; but often they leave it to others to supply a fuller conception of what is meant. . . .

During the present century . . . the catalogue of crimes has expanded. The laws today reach beyond the forbidden activities.

[1] From "A General View," by Walter Gellhorn, professor of law, Columbia University. In *The States and Subversion*, edited by Walter Gellhorn. Cornell University Press. Ithaca, New York. 1952. p359-80. Reprinted by permission.

They often touch as well those who advocate or teach the propriety of forbidden activities in any circumstances. . . .

Even more significant than this development has been an enlarged concern about groups as distinct from individuals. Traditionally the criminal law has dealt with the malefactor, the one who himself committed an offense. Departing from this tradition is the recent tendency to ascribe criminal potentialities to a body of persons (usually, though not invariably, the Communists) and to lay restraints upon any individual who can be linked with the group. This, of course, greatly widens the concept of subversive activities, because it results, in truth, in forgetting about activities altogether. It substitutes associations as the objects of the law's impact.

Since violence has not been the norm of politics within the states of this country, the abundance of penal statutes dealing with forcible assaults upon government may perhaps arouse wonder. Two explanations are immediately apparent.

First, criminal laws are adopted only rarely as a response to an existing crime wave. Rather, they prescribe the consequence of antisocial conduct should it occur, though everyone hopes it will not. Law expresses a community sense about evil. Embodying this sense in a formal utterance may in itself serve to reinforce the group ethic. Whatever discourages misdeeds is all to the good.

Second, the legislatures of many states may face somewhat the same problems and pressures at about the same time. When this happens, some of the legislatures may fail to analyze the issues with calm independence but may instead merely seize upon a conveniently available example. . . .

At times legislative ingenuity seems to be exercised not so much to protect the commonwealth against lawlessness as, in essence, to find new ways of expressing loathing. . . . Almost inescapable is the conclusion that at least some of the antisubversion, or anti-Communist, laws are not intrinsically justifiable as societal safeguards. They have been enacted because thus the legislators can demonstrate hatred of communism.

In part this satisfies a sincerely felt hunger for expression. In part it may merely satisfy a desire for personal advancement.

The instinct for political self-preservation has undoubtedly underlain some of the votes cast in recent years in support of purportedly anti-Communist legislation. . . . Only the most courageous legislator runs the political risk of casting a negative vote that can be interpreted as sympathy with communism. . . .

Nowhere has concern about subversive activities been more steadily manifest than in the educational process. Although only eighteen states specifically exclude subversive persons (variously defined) from employment in government service, twenty-six states bar them from teaching in public schools and state universities. Almost without exception the publicly supported school is a leading target, if not the primary target, of state legislative investigations into un-American activities. . . .

This is not the place to discuss at length the role of education in American society. Public opinion about the matter has not yet crystallized into a single fixed conviction. Some persons sincerely believe that the schools should propound only views that have already been approved; the demand that they instill a love of country is sometimes merely a subtle way of saying that they should not criticize the status quo. . . . On the other side is the feeling that schools should heighten their students' capacity to analyze problems, to organize and apply the pertinent fact materials, and to maintain a genuine open-mindedness, if not an active skepticism. . . . Being actively orthodox rather than open-mindedly inquiring has been the safer course for public educators. . . .

In late years the political identification of teachers, especially those at the college level, has been stressed even more than the character of what they taught. The policy that Communists should not be allowed to remain on faculties has gained wide acceptance despite the pleadings of the American Association of University Professors and a few other traditional upholders of academic freedom. . . .

The theory underlying the proscription of Communists as teachers rests on two propositions: first, that their political obligations include surrender of their intellectual freedom; and, second, that they will abuse their academic privileges by seeking to indoctrinate their students. Both of these propositions may be true. . . . But . . . their invariable truth has simply been assumed rather than tested in the various state investigations thus far held. By reiteration they have acquired the character of dogmas. This makes it impolitic to inquire into their soundness. . . .

There is, in any event, another aspect of the matter. Communists are generally believed to modify their asserted beliefs in order to meet the tactical needs of the immediate moment. Thus, for example, an historian might be called upon to distort historical facts in order to further some partisan effort. Although he might fully realize that his historical observations were spurious, he might nevertheless be willing (if a Communist) to be intellectually dishonest for his party's purposes. . . . It is especially in this sense . . . that the surrender of the mind would render a teacher unworthy of his profession.

Here again, the investigations of the states simply assert the existence rather than demonstrate the specific occurrence of this sort of impropriety. Full reliance has been placed on quotations from Lenin, from party writings of various kinds, and from Communist utterances in other days or contexts; these are used as though they equally reflected the active personal philosophy of every single Communist without the slightest modification or variation. Little effort has been made to show that a particular individual has behaved in an unprincipled manner. Evidence that an instructor is a Communist has not been regarded merely as justifying an inquiry by the appropriate academic authorities into what sort of teacher he is. Instead, it has been taken, standing quite alone, as conclusive proof that he has frittered away his intellectual freedom and is therefore no longer fit to teach. . . . As for the question of indoctrination, here again the state investigations have assumed rather than found that every Communist perverts his academic duties. . . . Rarely is a "disloyal" teacher charged with indoctrinating pupils with his hated ideas. His misconduct is simply assumed even though no proof of its existence can be brought forward. . . .

Pretty clearly the real opposition to a Communist as a teacher is that he is Communist rather than that he is a teacher of communism.

RÉSUMÉ OF STATE ANTI-SUBVERSIVE ACTIVITIES [2]

Two of the strongest antisubversion laws affecting teachers are New York's Feinberg Law and Maryland's Ober Act, both adopted in 1949. The Feinberg Law provides that no person who (a) advocates, (b) writes, prints, publishes or edits documents which advocate, (c) organizes, helps organize or becomes a member of a society which advocates the overthrow of government by force shall receive or remain in public employment. Any person dismissed on these grounds may petition within four months for an order to show cause and be heard in open court. The law gave power to the Board of Regents to adopt and enforce rules for removal of school employees disqualified by its provisions.

To give effect to the Feinberg Law, the New York State Education Department has distributed forms to all school boards on which to report whether they employ anyone with membership in a subversive organization. The Board of Regents is preparing a list of organizations it considers subversive; membership in any one of these will be prima facie evidence for disqualification.

The New York City Board of Education has ruled that a teacher who refuses to tell whether he is a member of the Communist party must be dismissed. It is the city's policy, however, to retain a teacher if he was formerly a party member but has decontaminated himself. The New York program to rid the schools of Communist teachers was commended to boards of education throughout the country by the McCarran subcommittee.

Under Maryland's Ober Act, public schools are required to fire any employee who aids, advises, or teaches by any means the overthrow of the constitutional form of the Federal Government or the government of the state of Maryland by revolution, force or violence, or who is a member of a group advocating such action. The law established a new post of assistant attorney general for its state-wide administration. . . .

[2] From "Red Teachers and Educational Freedom," by Helen Shaffer, research editor. *Editorial Research Reports.* 1, no6:108-14. February 11, 1953. Reprinted by permission.

A United Press survey in mid-January disclosed scattered activity in the states complying with recommendations of the McCarran subcommittee for increased effort to banish communism from the schools. The Michigan legislature is considering legislation to create a state un-American activities committee to check up on educational institutions. The Pennsylvania Department of Justice is investigating Red activity in the public schools. State authorities in Wisconsin are inquiring into circumstances surrounding a speech made under sponsorship of the Labor Youth League by a *Daily Worker* editor. The Ohio Un-American Activities Commission is engaged in an investigation of institutions of higher learning and three Ohio State University graduate assistants and instructors have been cited for contempt after refusing to answer questions put by the commission.

Teachers are required to take loyalty oaths in some thirty states, but many of these are the regular oaths of office prescribed by state constitutions or long-standing statutes. The tendency in recent years has been to require a negative oath, disclaiming affiliation with subversive groups or participation in pro-Communist activity. Thirteen states now require oaths of this kind. . . .

Loyalty oath laws usually apply to all public employees. A few states extend the requirement to teachers in private schools. At least eight states require a promise from the teacher that he will inculcate loyalty and patriotism in the children. The Rhode Island oath reads in part:

I pledge myself to neglect no opportunity to teach the children committed to my care loyalty to nation and state, honor to the flag, obedience to law and government, respect for public servants entrusted . . . with the functions of government, faith in government by the people, fealty to the civic principles of freedom, equal rights and human brotherhood, and the duty of every citizen to render service for the common welfare . . .

As a teacher of the public's children, I have no right, either in school hours, or in the presence of my pupils out of school hours, to express opinions that conflict with honor to my country, loyalty to American ideals, and obedience to and respect for the laws of nation and state.

Teachers in most states have legal protection against unjust dismissal under tenure laws which provide for notice, statement of reasons, and opportunity for self-defense prior to severance from their jobs. The tenure laws of half a dozen states prohibit dismissal for political reasons, but several of these states have other laws requiring dismissal for membership in the Communist party or Communist-front organizations. Roughly 1,400 teachers under direct jurisdiction of the national government are subject to the regular Federal loyalty check.

Typical of the forces for and against teacher oath laws were those arrayed before the Pennsylvania legislature last year when such a measure was under debate. Supporting the bill were the American Legion, Veterans of Foreign Wars and Amvets. [Although veteran groups have led in pressing for loyalty oath legislation, the Oregon Veterans Legislative Committee, representing the five leading national veterans organizations, decided this year against asking the legislature for additional loyalty oaths on the grounds that the existing affirmative oaths of office were sufficient and "sincere educators and public officials are best qualified to enforce loyalty laws."] Petitioning against it were 1,500 educators from fifteen state institutions, among them Milton Eisenhower, president of Pennsylvania State; Harold Stassen, then president of the University of Pennsylvania, and the heads of Bryn Mawr and Bucknell.

The United States Supreme Court has upheld the right of the states to require disclaimer oaths from teachers in several recent decisions. In the 6-3 decision on the Feinberg Law, March 3, 1952, the Court rejected contentions that the statute was an 'bridgment of free speech and that it took away liberty or property without due process of law. The majority held that states have the rightful power to protect immature minds from propaganda disseminated by public employees whom the pupils are expected to regard as authorities. [The Ober law of Maryland was upheld by the Supreme Court on April 12, 1952, in a case which challenged a provision requiring candidates for state and city office to take a loyalty oath.] Dissenting opinions of three justices (Black, Douglas, Frankfurter) held that the New

York law restricts academic freedom and establishes the principle of guilt by association.

The Supreme Court declared the Oklahoma loyalty-oath law unconstitutional last December 15 because it banned employment of teachers who had been associated within the previous five years with any group listed as subversive by the United States Attorney General. In this case a unanimous Court held that such a requirement afforded no protection to individuals who had innocently joined such groups.

NEW YORK INVESTIGATIONS
AND LEGISLATION [3]

In *Free Speech in the United States,* Zechariah Chafee remarks that probing committees seem indigenous to New York. The first one . . . was created in 1780 to detect and defeat conspiracies of Loyalists. Professor Chafee was writing with special reference to the activities of the Lusk committee in 1919-1920. Since that time two additional New York legislative investigations of seditious or subversive activities have been added to the record.

Thus thirty years have produced three legislative investigations of "subversive" activities. All have devoted some attention to the schools, but only the last concentrated upon the schools. During the same period legislative concern over dangerous activity on the part of employees in governmental or educational institutions has found expression in other ways. . . . From the short-lived Lusk laws of 1921 to the Feinberg Law of 1949, a number of legislative proposals of one kind or another have been directed at the suppression or elimination of dangerous persons. Most of these proposed measures have been aimed at teachers or other educational employees. Many of the proposals have not been enacted but several have, the most important being the Ives Loyalty Oath Law of 1934, the Devany Law of 1939, and the Feinberg Law of 1949.

[3] From the Introduction to *Loyalty and Legislative Action,* by Lawrence H. Chamberlain, dean of Columbia College. Cornell University Press. Ithaca, New York. 1951. p 1-5. Reprinted by permission.

NEW YORK'S FEINBERG LAW [4]

The recent Supreme Court ruling upholding the constitutionality of the New York State Feinberg Law . . . [in] *Adler et al.* v. *Board of Education of the City of New York* . . . makes available to all states a judicially approved procedure for the removal of Communist and other subversive teachers from the public schools. It goes one step further by spelling out the fundamental relationship of the public school teacher to his employer, the state. . . .

The Feinberg Law . . . was passed with the express purpose of strengthening two existing antisubversive measures. In 1917 New York State had enacted Section 3021 of the Education Law which provided for the removal of any public school employee who engaged in "treasonable or seditious" acts or utterances. Twenty-two years later Section 12-a of the New York Civil Law (the Devany Law) was passed in order to disqualify from the civil service and the education system anyone who advocated, or who was a member of any organization which advocated, the overthrow of the Federal or state governments by force, violence or any unlawful means. . . . No proceedings were ever taken under these two laws.

Then, in 1949, the Feinberg Law was passed. It begins with a lengthy preamble stating that, despite existing legislation, members of subversive groups, particularly the Communist party and its affiliated organizations, have infiltrated into the school system. In order to prevent the dissemination of subversive propaganda among children of tender years, the law sets up a series of directives for the Board of Regents, the agency in charge of the state public school system. First, the Board is required to promulgate and enforce rules for the removal of superintendents of schools, teachers and other school employees who violate Section 3021 of the Education Law and Section 12-a of the Civil Service Law. Then, "after inquiry, and after such notice and hearing as may be appropriate," the Board must issue a list of subversive organizations—those that advocate, advise, teach or

[4] From "Recent Supreme Court Decisions: The State, the Teacher and Subversive Activity," by Isadore Starr, social studies teacher, Brooklyn Technical High School, in New York, and author of *Human Rights in the United States*. *Social Education*. 16:309-11. November 1952. Reprinted by permission.

embrace the doctrine that the government of the United States or of any state shall be overthrown by force, violence or unlawful means. Federal lists may be utilized for this purpose, and the listing may be revised from time to time. Membership in any of these organizations is to "constitute prima facie evidence of disqualification for appointment to or retention in any office or position in the public schools of the state." Lastly, the Board is required to report annually to the legislature on the means taken for the enforcement of the law.

Two court actions were immediately instituted against the law. . . . The main contention was that it represented an abridgment of freedom of speech and assembly as guaranteed by the due process clause of the Fourteenth Amendment. And, in addition, it was pointed out that making membership in an organization listed as subversive an automatic ground for dismissal was a denial of procedural due process.

The opponents of the law triumphed in the Supreme Court of New York State, but they lost in all the appellate courts. The case that reached the United States Supreme Court was an action seeking a declaratory judgment stating that the Feinberg Law and Section 12-a of the Civil Service Law are unconstitutional violations of the due process clause of the Fourteenth Amendment. . . .

Justice Minton wrote the majority opinion of the Court—it was a 6-3 decision—sustaining the law as a constitutional exercise of the state's police power "to protect the schools from pollution and thereby to defend its own existence." The very heart of the majority's reasoning is set forth in the following paragraph:

A teacher works in a sensitive area in a schoolroom. There he shapes the attitude of young minds towards the society in which they live. In this, the state has a vital concern. It must preserve the integrity of the schools. That the school authorities have the right and the duty to screen the officials, teachers and employees as to their fitness to maintain the integrity of the schools as a part of ordered society, cannot be doubted. One's associates, past and present, as well as one's conduct, may properly be considered in determining fitness and loyalty. From time immemorial, one's reputation has been determined in part by the company he keeps. In the employment of officials and teachers of the school system, the state may properly inquire into the company they keep, and we know of no rule, constitutional or otherwise, that prevents the state, when determining the fitness and loyalty of such persons, from considering the organizations and persons with whom they associate.

With this as their basic tenet, the majority finds no constitutional infirmity in the law. Since a state has the right to impose "reasonable terms" on its educational employees, New York has the power of denying jobs in its school system to those who advocate or belong to organizations that advocate the overthrow of the government by force, violence or unlawful means. There is no abridgment of expression and assembly, because those who refuse to work for New York State under the terms of the Feinberg Law can "go elsewhere" and exercise their right to "assemble, think and believe as they will."

MARYLAND'S OBER LAW [5]

Frank B. Ober played the leading role in the drama of Maryland politics in 1949. . . . Ober's prominence on the political stage resulted from his service as chairman of a commission brought into existence by resolution of the state legislature in 1948 to prepare a program of anti-Communist legislation. . . . The law which the legislature adopted, adhering closely to the commission's recommendations, became known as the Ober Act. . . .

Ober's concern about Communist influence in educational institutions was given pointed expression . . . when he refused to contribute to the Law School fund of Harvard University, of which he is an alumnus. His act of protest, Ober wrote to President James Conant, was prompted by the fact that two members of the Harvard faculty had participated in meetings sponsored by organizations commonly accused of following the Communist party line. . . .

The Ober commission devoted great care to what it conceived to be its task—the drafting of legislation which would effectively suppress an evil. . . . The professional work of drafting the law

[5] From "Maryland: The Ober Anti-Communist Law," by William B. Prendergast, assistant professor of government, United States Naval Academy. In *The States and Subversion*, edited by Walter Gellhorn. Cornell University Press. Ithaca, New York. 1952. p 140-83. Reprinted by permission.

was performed with great skill. . . . The commission's avowed aim was to "destroy communism without destroying Americanism." To that end it embodied in the law it proposed certain provisions designed to guard against the use of investigative power for character assassination. Because of "the criticism that has so often been made against some legislative committees," the Ober commission refrained from recommending the establishment of an un-American activities committee in the state. Investigations, it decided, should be conducted by grand juries and by a special assistant attorney general, who was charged with the duty of enforcing the act. . . .

The Ober commission submitted to the governor on December 30, 1948, a draft of a proposed statute to be known as the Subversive Activities Act of 1949 and a report justifying the proposal. In large part the statute was a synthesis of the Smith Act, portions of the Mundt-Nixon Bill, and the loyalty program established for employees of the national government by executive order in 1947. It was described by the American Civil Liberties Union as the most sweeping measure of its type enacted in 1949. . . . A carbon copy of a large part of the Ober Act was placed on the statute books of Mississippi one year later with the enactment of that state's Subversive Activities Act of 1950.

In its criminal sections the Ober Act attacks the Communist movement by describing its characteristics rather than by naming it. The terms of the law single out two objectives commonly attributed to American Communists—the overthrow of government by violence, and the establishment of a puppet government in the United States. To prevent the forcible overthrow of government, the Ober Act declares felonious (1) acts intended to have such a result, (2) words advocating such acts if uttered "under such circumstances as to constitute a clear and present danger to the security of the United States or of the State of Maryland," and (3) participation in any organization advocating the forcible overthrow of government. . . .

The act makes criminal participation in a foreign-controlled organization seeking to establish in place of the existing national or state governments "any form of government the direction and control of which is to be vested in, or exercised by or under, the domination or control of any foreign government, organization, or individual. . . ."

Subversive organizations and foreign subversive organizations are banned by the Ober Act. . . .

The foregoing criminal provisions constitute one of the two major divisions of the Ober Act. The other is a loyalty section aimed at excluding subversive persons from the public payroll as well as from the payroll of any private educational institution receiving financial support from the state. Declaring subversives ineligible for appointment to, or employment in, any governmental office within the state, the act provides for a somewhat flexible loyalty program. Every public job holder at the time the law becomes effective was required to submit a written statement that he was not subversive. . . . Appointees to office after the act has become effective are to be screened for loyalty. Each appointing authority is directed to establish its own procedure for this purpose, no specifications being laid down in the law to guide state agencies. Appointments can be made only after it is established by such procedure that "no reasonable grounds" exist to believe that a prospective appointee is subversive.

One holding an appointive position in the service of the state is to be discharged if "reasonable grounds on all the evidence" exist for the belief that the job holder is subversive. . . .

Finally, the act fixes its sights on subversive teachers by requiring all private institutions of learning receiving any state funds to report the procedures adopted by them for the detection of subversives in their employ and the steps taken to terminate such employment. The penalty for noncompliance is denial of state aid to the uncooperative institution. It was no secret that Johns Hopkins University was the target of this provision. . .

The private educational institutions in the state which receive public funds have filed statements certifying that their employees are not subversive. The presidents of the smaller institutions vouch for their faculties and administrative staffs on the basis of their personal knowledge of the employees concerned. Johns Hopkins University appointed a faculty committee to determine whether the procedures used in selecting faculty and administrative employees included adequate safeguards against infiltration by subversive individuals. The committee's investigation and affirmative answer to the question were accepted as compliance with the requirements of the Ober Act. . . .

The loyalty program envisaged by the Ober Act is similar in some respects to that of the national government. Here again the act did not follow an uncharted path. Twenty-nine states had earlier imposed some sort of loyalty requirement for public employees, eight additional states (including Maryland) enacted a loyalty law in 1949, and Mississippi joined the ranks in 1950. In most of the states all that is demanded is the execution of a declaration of loyalty by those holding a public position. Only in Maryland, Mississippi, and New Hampshire does the law impose a state-wide loyalty program involving more than securing affidavits from the employees affected.

Courts which have passed on loyalty measures offer little comfort to the opponents of such devices. The judiciary has in most instances declined to intervene to prevent the execution of loyalty programs or to stay dismissals for disloyalty. Maryland's Court of Appeals and the United States Supreme Court have upheld the loyalty declaration which the Ober Act requires of candidates for public office. It is unlikely that any part of the law's loyalty program can be successfully challenged on constitutional grounds, although the courts might refuse to sanction arbitrary applications of it in individual cases. . . .

The writer is unable to discern any threat to academic freedom or any infringement of a right that can reasonably be asserted in barring from public employment those who are unwilling to say that they do not advocate the overthrow of government by force or the establishment of a puppet government in the United States. It may be granted that some loyalty oaths are highly objectionable. The oath demanded of Rhode Island's teachers obliging them to teach a specific theory of government, the oath required of Georgia's officeholders disavowing "sympathy" for any of the doctrines of communism would be cases in point. Such oaths, strictly interpreted, and applied, restrict free inquiry. But the declaration demanded by the Ober Act restrains no one from seeking or speaking truth. . . .

The Ober Act provides for a flexible loyalty program, granting to the several thousand appointing officers within the state
the power to establish procedural rules for determining loyalty.
. . . Allowing each appointing officer to adopt his own procedures for testing loyalty and to determine who is loyal and
who is not may produce confusing variation, erratic and uncertain
standards, error and injustice. . . .

The imposition of rough standards of loyalty forged by
political leaders upon educational institutions is an ominous
possibility under the Ober Act. No private school may receive
state funds unless it has adopted procedures to determine whether
subversive individuals are in its employ and has taken steps to
terminate such employment. A lever is thereby provided by
which small-minded politicians may impose their standards of
loyalty upon some of the schools of the state if they are disposed
to do so. The only penalty imposed upon an institution which
refuses to carry out this provision of the law is denial of financial
support from the state treasury. To Johns Hopkins University,
which derives about 1 per cent of its income from the state, the
penalty which the law imposes directly would not be severe; to
St. John's College, which depends on the state treasury for one-
seventh of its revenue, the result would be catastrophic. . . .

The need for the Ober Act was never satisfactorily demonstrated by its proponents. . . . The only Communist known to
have been on the public payroll was a kindergarten teacher in
the Baltimore school system, who was dismissed in 1948. Since
the passage of the Ober Act, three "probables" have been found
in the school system, all of whom were removed without recourse
to the Act.

THE PENNSYLVANIA LOYALTY ACT [6]

Introduction of Senate Bill Number 27 on January 15, 1951,
by Senator Albert R. Pechan began a bitter, prolonged, and
widely publicized debate which culminated in the enactment of
the Pennsylvania Loyalty Act on December 22, 1951. . . . Sena-

[6] From "A Report on the Pennsylvania Loyalty Act," by Clark Byse, professor
of law, University of Pennsylvania. *University of Pennsylvania Law Review*. 101:
480-508. January 1953. Reprinted by permission.

tor Pechan's original bill contained only two sections and required every employee of the commonwealth or any of its political subdivisions to file a written statement under oath or affirmation that he was not a subversive person as defined in the bill. By the time the bill was finally enacted, it had been amended nine times, had grown to seventeen sections [thirty-four pages] and embraced a variety of topics in addition to the original requirement of a loyalty oath from public employees.

Although the new provisions added in the amendment process drastically changed Senator Pechan's original proposal, the bill was known throughout as the "Loyalty Oath Bill" and public discussion and debate generally took the form of support of or opposition to a loyalty oath. The emphasis on the oath aspects of the bill, the numerous revisions and amendments as the measure passed through the legislative mill, and the omnibus character of the act finally adopted militated against public knowledge and understanding of its terms. . . .

The Pennsylvania Loyalty Act contains five major provisions: (1) Every employee of, and applicant for employment by, the Commonwealth of Pennsylvania or of any of its political subdivisions (including school districts) is required to swear to or affirm his loyalty. (2) Although an oath is not required of persons holding state or local elective offices at the time the act became effective, every person who thereafter becomes a candidate for "state, district, county, or local public office" is required to file with his nomination papers a statement under oath or affirmation that he is not a "subversive person" as defined in the act. (3) Any employee of the commonwealth or of any of its political subdivisions who, after due hearing, is determined to be a subversive person shall be discharged. (4) Any applicant for employment by the commonwealth or any of its political subdivisions shall not be employed if he is a subversive person or if "on all the evidence there is reasonable doubt concerning his loyalty to the government of the United States or the Commonwealth of Pennsylvania." (5) No public funds shall be paid to any state-aided institution of learning unless the institution annually files with the governor a written report setting forth what procedures the institution has adopted to determine whether it has reason to believe that any subversive persons are in its employ and what steps, if any, have been or are being taken to terminate such employment. The report also shall set forth unequivocally that the institution has no reason to believe that any subversive persons are in its employ. . . .

The Act . . . [became] effective on March 1, 1952. On or before that date thousands of state and local employees throughout the commonwealth executed the required loyalty statement. . . . To date there have been no perjury prosecutions. The only tangible results of the oath requirement have been: (a) a feeling of resentment on the part of many loyal teachers and employees who object to being singled out and forced to take an oath not required of other citizens; (b) the resignation of an employee of the Philadelphia City Planning Commission who, after executing the loyalty statement, resigned his position in protest against the requirement; and (c) the discharge of three teachers, a social worker, three doctors, and a nurse who refused to execute the required statement. . . . There was no suggestion by anyone that any of these individuals was in any way subversive or disloyal. . . .

Section 13 of the Pennsylvania Loyalty Act prohibits payment of public funds "to any state-aided institution of learning not a part of the public school system" (the four principal state-aided educational institutions are the Pennsylvania State College, Temple University, University of Pennsylvania, and University of Pittsburgh) which fails to file with the governor "a written report setting forth what procedures the institution has adopted to determine whether it has reason to believe that any subversive persons are in its employ and what steps, if any, have been or are being taken to terminate such employment. The report shall also unequivocally set forth that the institution has no reason to believe any subversive persons are in its employ." The report must be approved by the governor before public funds can be paid.

The version of the act originally passed by the senate on March 28 required a loyalty oath not only from employees of the commonwealth or of any of its political subdivisions but as well from employees of "any college or school which receives state aid." In April 1951, representatives of the four principal state-aided educational institutions met in Harrisburg with legislators interested in loyalty legislation. The educational leaders emphasized the objectionable features of the oath requirement contained in the bill the senate had passed. They pointed to the experience of the University of California as an example of the harm that can result from ill-advised loyalty oath requirements. They urged that the objective of keeping subversives out of their institutions could better be achieved by delegating the task to the institutions—as had been done in Maryland by the Ober Law—than by the blanket oath requirement of the bill passed by the senate. When the House Committee on State Government, to which the senate bill had been referred, reported the bill out in May, the requirement of an oath from employees from state-aided educational institutions had been deleted and present Section 13 had been incorporated.

ILLINOIS: THE BROYLES COMMISSION [7]

During the last decade and a half the Illinois legislature has launched two investigations of alleged subversive activities. In the first, attention was focused solely upon the University of Chicago. The second investigation, although authorized to engage in a wider scope of inquiry, also concentrated upon the University of Chicago, with ancillary attention paid to the recently formed Roosevelt College. Aside from this surface similarity the contrast between the two investigations is marked. The so-called "Walgreen" investigation in 1935 was touched off by widely published charges of Charles Walgreen, owner of one of Chicago's leading retail drug chains, that his niece had been indoctrinated with communistic ideologies by certain members of the University of Chicago faculty. Lengthy public hearings conducted by a committee of five state senators resulted in four of the five senators' concluding that there were no Communists on the faculty of the University of Chicago, that the faculty made

[7] From article by E. Houston Harsha, research associate at the University of Chicago Law School, currently trial attorney, Antitrust Division, United States Department of Justice. In *The States and Subversion*, edited by Walter Gellhorn. Cornell University Press. Ithaca, New York. 1952. p54-6, 129. Reprinted by permission.

no effort to indoctrinate students with communism, and that existing sedition laws of Illinois were adequate to restrain advocacy of violent overthrow of the government. In contrast, the Seditious Activities Investigation Commission, popularly known as the Broyles commission, devoted two years to secret investigation of subversive activities throughout the state, then publicly investigated alleged subversion at the University of Chicago and Roosevelt College, and, while formulating no conclusions as to whether Communists were on the faculty of either school or students were indoctrinated with communism, issued a statement in June 1949, condemning conditions at the two schools and recommending that tax exemptions be withdrawn from them both. . . .

With respect to teachers, the majority of the Broyles commission recommended that "any teacher or professor who refuses to resign from known Communist or Communist-front organizations . . . be dismissed from the faculty of any tax-exempt, or tax-supported institution of learning."

CALIFORNIA: THE TENNEY COMMITTEE [8]

Prior to 1940 legislative regulation of subversive activities in California had been confined to a criminal syndicalism act, a Red Flag law, and general criminal statutes dealing with treason, rebellion, insurrections, and riots. During the decade of the 1940's, although a few statutes were added to the list, the emphasis shifted from legislative regulation to legislative investigation and exposure as a means of combating subversive activities. . . .

The Fact-Finding Committee on Un-American Activities under the chairmanship of Senator Jack B. Tenney (the Tenney committee) operated continuously from 1941 to 1949. . . . During 1941 and 1942 the committee heard a few witnesses regarding alleged radical activities in the schools of the state. In its 1943 report the committee stated that . . . "your committee is convinced that communism is not being *taught* in the universities, or in any part of our public schools throughout California.

[8] From "California: Regulation and Investigation of Subversive Activities," by Edward L. Barrett, Jr., professor of law, University of California. In *The States and Subversion*, edited by Walter Gellhorn. Cornell University Press. Ithaca, New York. 1952. p 1-21. Reprinted by permission.

Your committee, however, is convinced, that . . . there are a considerable number of instructors and faculty members who are either active members of the Communist party or whose positions relegate them to the role of 'fellow traveler.' "

In August 1943, a Writers' Congress was announced to be held on the campus of the University of California at Los Angeles . . . under the joint sponsorship of U.C.L.A. and the Hollywood Writers' Mobilization. In September Senator Tenney sent a fifteen-page report to President Sproul of the University of California charging that the Congress was Communist-inspired. . . . Tenney's charges were denied by the university officials responsible for the congress. Tenney then publicly threatened to order an investigation by his committee if the congress was not canceled. The congress was held as scheduled. . . .

In the 1945 report the committee gave three pages to telling of the starting of a workers' education school—The Peoples Educational Center—in Los Angeles in 1943. This report . . . concluded that it was "inspired and controlled by the Communists." At Los Angeles in January 1946 the committee . . . questioned various members of the faculty of the University of California at Los Angeles . . . regarding their participation in the work of the center. . . .

A considerable portion of the January 1946 hearing was devoted not to the center but to the University of California at Los Angeles. Six members of the faculty were called for interrogation. . . . These hearings were reported at some length in the committee's 1947 report under the heading, "University Professors and Communist Schools." In hearings held in Oakland in September 1946, the committee took testimony regarding alleged Communist control of the California Labor School, a San Francisco institution, and regarding the professors of the University of California at Berkeley who were sponsors or otherwise associated with this school.

Over the years the committee sponsored a rather large number of bills in the state legislature. It succeeded, however, in having but a few of them enacted into law. . . . In 1947 the committee introduced a series of eight bills designed to prevent the teaching of controversial subjects in the elementry schools and to increase the legislative control over the selection of textbooks and educational policies. Of these eight only one became law. . . .

In 1949 the committee introduced a comprehensive program of legislation designed . . . to "isolate, expose and move from positions of power and influence persons who are a dangerous menace to our freedom and security." This program included bills broadly defining communism and Communist; making it a misdemeanor to teach any of the "isms" except Americanism upon school property with the intent to indoctrinate the pupils; requiring candidates for public office and all state employees to subscribe to special loyalty oaths; requiring subversive organizations to keep written records of their meetings. . . . A constitutional amendment was proposed to take from the regents of the University of California and give to the legislature the power to ensure the loyalty of officers and employees of the university. It was to forestall the enactment of this measure that the regents imposed their now famous loyalty oath. . . .

This legislative program was vigorously attacked and defended. Seven of the bills passed the senate by large majorities. They were defeated in the assembly only at the last moment as the climax of a bitter fight over the continuation of the Tenney committee which . . . led to the resignation of Tenney from the committee. [The committee, however, has continued in operation up to the present time, with the schools still a major target for investigation.—Ed.]

RECENT DEVELOPMENTS IN CALIFORNIA [9]

Prior to . . . March [1952] the committee [California Senate Committee on Un-American Activities] conducted numerous public and closed hearings concerning Communist infiltration in the educational institutions of California. Last March the committee had a meeting at the University of Southern California, which . . . was attended by all the presidents of the colleges and universities in the southern part of California. . . .

[9] From testimony of Richard E. Combs, attorney and chief counsel for the California Senate Committee on Un-American Activities, March 19, 1953. In *Subversive Influence in the Educational Process;* hearings, part V, March 19, 24-25, 1953, before a subcommittee of the Senate Judiciary Committee. 83d Congress, 1st session. The Committee. Washington 25, D.C. 1953. p606-8.

On the 24th of the following June, we had a similar meeting at the University of San Francisco attended by all the college and university presidents in the northern part of the state. A week thereafter, all colleges joined in a cooperative plan to combat Communist infiltration.

About a hundred faculty members have been removed from the faculties as a result of this plan since the 24th of . . . June [1952]. . . .

In addition to that . . . the committee deemed it expedient to indicate to the university administrators the necessity, particularly in the larger institutions, of employing full-time people who had had a practical experience in the field of counter-Communist activities, ex-FBI agents, and ex-Navy and military intelligence men. That has been followed.

UNIVERSITY OF CALIFORNIA POLICY ON INVESTIGATION TESTIMONY [10]

To assist the faculty members in making their decisions, the Committee on Academic Freedom of the University of California has submitted to the Northern Section of the Academic Senate at Berkeley a verbose report reducible to a single word: "cooperate."

"The Committee on Academic Freedom believes that a member of the faculty of the University of California is under obligation to testify in a cooperative manner in inquiries lawfully conducted by legally constituted state and Federal investigating committees," this group advises. "Refusal to testify could set in motion a series of events which could result in dismissal from the faculty." . . .

However, the committee suggests, members of the faculty "should also be assured of protection of their university status if, as a result of testifying in a cooperative manner, they are subjected to persecution." . . .

Refusal to testify can be considered "contempt" and the regents of the university are required by law to discharge a person

[10] From "Unhappy Decision," by Godfrey Lehman, San Francisco correspondent for *Frontier*, contributor to various business publications. *Frontier.* 4:2. July 1953. Reprinted by permission.

who is guilty of contempt. Once so discharged he can never be re-employed by the university. . . .

The committee now cautions that there is "no question but that state committees have been granted extremely wide powers, and if these powers are not used with wisdom and with restraint they could result in invasions of rights which are protected and guaranteed by the Constitution." Then the report adds that if a faculty member feels the abuses are in conflict with the Constitution, "the faculty member as a citizen may feel compelled to resist them in order that they may be tested in the courts. In this matter a person's conscience must be the ultimate guide."

THE CANWELL COMMITTEE AND THE
UNIVERSITY OF WASHINGTON [11]

On January 22, 1949, the Board of Regents of the university took final action in six tenure cases which for more than six months had been before various faculty and administrative officers and agencies. The action of the Regents consisted of the dismissal, as of February 1, of three professors and the retention of three others on two-year probation subject to the requirement that they sign and file with the president of the university affidavits that they are not now members of the Communist party.

The vote of the regents represented the University of Washington's solution of a problem that for many years has disturbed not only this university but higher education in America generally. The cases from which the decision emerged represented, first, the university's effort to face squarely, and to answer questions surrounding, the effect of Communist party membership on the qualifications of a teacher. . . .

The question of whether members of the Communist party should be allowed to teach on the faculty of an American university . . . is one that has caused difficulty in many institutions, seriously affecting both the internal and external relations of colleges and universities throughout America. The problem is an

[11] From Introduction to *Communism and Academic Freedom*, the record of the tenure cases at the University of Washington, by President Raymond B. Allen. University of Washington Press. Seattle. 1949. p 11-19. Reprinted by permission.

extremely delicate one, for it involves fundamental questions of academic freedom, and it is one which must be faced without the benefit of conclusive judicial findings on the nature of the Communist party. The problem is one which, in my view, has been too long neglected by universities everywhere and which, even when it has been examined, has been touched only on its periphery and never before faced head on nor subject to definitive study with full academic procedures and safeguards.

There needs to be constant scrutiny of the application of principles of academic freedom as these principles may apply in specific situations. There appears to be a need, too, for a closer examination of the higher responsibilities, obligations, and duties of the college teacher as they are weighed in the balance against his privileges, rights, and immunities. . . .

With this thought in mind the University of Washington's experience in dealing with these cases perhaps has greater significance than the solution of an immediate and pressing problem of the university itself. It may have the additional virtue of providing a starting point, at least, for other educational institutions faced with similar problems. . . .

The university's problems, while in no sense different from those which might have arisen elsewhere, came into being against a background of the liberal thought and action of the Pacific Northwest. The tenure cases emerged from this special background. For many years the university had been charged with being a hotbed of communism and the harbor of what was called "a nest of Communist professors." The many years of charges concerning Communist activity at the university and elsewhere in the state of Washington culminated in 1947 in the establishment by the state legislature of a Joint Legislative Fact-Finding Committee on Un-American Activities (popularly known as the Canwell Committee). This committee was similar to the Committee on Un-American Activities of the national House of Representatives and to legislative committees in other states. The committee was charged with inquiring into alleged subversive activities and objectives of individuals and organizations in the state of Washington, and was asked to report its findings to the next session of the legislature. The committee was instructed by the legislature to give special attention to Communist party activities that might affect "the functioning of any state agency, unemployment relief, and other forms of public assistance, educational institutions of this state supported in whole or in part by state funds." The second investigation undertaken by the legislative committee had as its subject alleged Communist activities on the University of Washington campus.

After some weeks of preliminary investigation, the committee held an open public hearing in Seattle starting on July 19, 1948, and lasting for one week. Throughout its investigation and hearings the university attempted to cooperate with this committee. Contrary to the impression that was encouraged in some quarters, by direct assertion and by insinuation, that the university administration had some mysterious "understanding" with the committee, the university's cooperation consisted, simply, of providing pertinent information on request from official files and from the knowledge of university personnel. Members of the university staff were urged to give facts as they knew them, and I asked those persons who were subpoenaed by the committee to be straightforward and frank in their testimony. For the most part, cooperation in this respect was furnished by practically all members of the university staff from whom information was sought.

It should be said also that in the open committee hearings no effort was made by committee members to elicit testimony on the political or social views of faculty members other than those who, for some concrete reason, were believed to be, or to have been, members of the Communist party. It is to the credit of the committee that it limited its inquiry to those situations where there was an actual question of Communist party membership.

In the hearings of the legislative committee ten members of the university faculty, all enjoying tenure under university rules, were named as being or having been members of the Communist party. Two of the ten flatly denied any association with the party. Five admitted past membership but denied present membership. The three others refused to testify as to past or present membership in the Communist party. (There were approximately seven hundred full-time members of the University faculty and about the same number of part-time and subfaculty members.)

Following the open hearings of the legislative committee, and after the information elicited by the committee had been studied carefully by the university administration, complaints were filed with the university faculty Committee on Tenure and Academic Freedom against six members of the faculty by Dean Edward H. Lauer of the College of Arts and Sciences. The six respondents included the three faculty members who had refused to testify as to past or present membership in the Communist party and three of those who had admitted past membership but denied present membership. Following the filing of complaints by Dean Lauer on September 8, 1948, and subsequent to formal replies by the six respondents, the faculty Committee on Tenure and Academic Freedom began its closed hearings in the cases on October 27, 1948. The hearings, lasting thirty-three sessions, were closed December 15, 1948. Testimony was taken from seventy-three witnesses. . . .

In the cases of the three faculty members who had refused to testify before the legislative committee as to Communist party membership, the first charge in each case was, "Respondent is and for many years past has been a member of the Communist party." This charge was not brought against the other three respondents. In two cases . . . all charges other than that relating to present and past membership in the Communist party were dropped in order to present a simple and clear-cut issue. . . .

The faculty committee . . . report was submitted to me on January 7, 1949, and transmitted to the Board of Regents on January 8, 1949. Under date of January 17, I transmitted to the Board a memorandum analyzing the committee's report and giving my findings and recommendations. . . .

The members of the Board of Regents met on January 22, 1949. The Board, with all members in attendance, then conducted its own hearing, listening to several hours of arguments of counsel for the respondents and to a statement by one of the respondents. . . . At the conclusion of the hearing, the Regents, in executive session, took the following action . . . :

The Board of Regents voted to adopt the President's recommendations for the dismissal of Messrs. Butterworth, Phillips, and Gundlach from the faculty of the University of Washington as of February 1, 1949.

The Board voted to adopt the President's recommendations against dismissal of Messrs. Jacobs, Eby, and Ethel, subject to the following conditions:

(a) That these men shall severally sign and file affidavits that they are not now members of the Communist party, and have not been members of the Communist party since the respective dates stated in their testimony before the faculty Tenure Committee. Failure to file such affidavits with the president of the university prior to February 1, 1949, shall result in immediate dismissal.

(b) That Messrs. Jacobs, Eby, and Ethel be further placed on probation for a period of two years.

When the regents had made their ruling, the university's procedures in this vital matter had run their full course. Professors Jacobs, Eby, and Ethel transmitted to me the affidavits requested by the Board. The difficult decision had been made.

THE LEGISLATURE AND THE UNIVERSITY
OF COLORADO [12]

An attempt to discredit the governor of Colorado by claiming his state university harbored "communistic, subversive professors" failed last March, but only after a month-long storm in that state's education and politics. Center of the controversy was the University of Colorado's top-secret report on "subversive" professors, which Governor Dan Thornton had ordered compiled but refused to make public.

Political enemies of Thornton, headed by State Senator Morton G. Wyatt [Democrat] used information secretly obtained from the report to attack Thornton and his appointee, Colorado University President, Robert L. Stearns. After Stearns had declared there were no "subversives" on the university faculty, Wyatt named three . . . and demanded they be fired. The speech

[12] From "Colorado Senate Feuds Defame Three Teachers," news story. *Harvard Crimson,* Fifth Annual Academic Freedom Report. p M3. June 10, 1953. Reprinted by permission.

. . . led Thornton supporters to rush to the aid of the university, while supporters of civil liberties demanded that the two-year-old report, compiled by former FBI agents, be either released or destroyed. Its six copies, however, still lie locked in a safe in the governor's office.

The dispute was the year's most clear-cut example of use of the "Communists-in-education" issue in state political fights.

The 126-page report is supposed to include the names of at least eleven professors who are past or present members of organizations on the Attorney-General's list of subversive organizations.

THE "SECRET REPORT" ON COLORADO
UNIVERSITY [13]

During . . . [the University of Colorado's] run-in with Senator Morton Wyatt of Lamar . . . the Republican members of the Board of Regents met in the governor's office with Republican legislators . . . and . . . gave those attending a statistical summary of the report on the investigation of the faculty which was made for the regents about two years ago. This report never has been made public. Here are the statistics:

Number of faculty investigated—15

Number cleared without report to the Board of Regents because of no evidence—4

Number of cases reported and cleared by the Regents after investigation—3

Number investigated and no longer in the employ of the University—8

Total—15

The Republican regents also informed the legislators that "all student organizations that have elsewhere been affiliated with subversive groups have been denied charters at the university and that at least two groups shown to have Communist leanings elsewhere have had their charters revoked and no longer exist on the campus."

[13] From "From Where We're Sitting," editorial. *The Colorado Alumnus*. 43:30. June 1953. Reprinted by permission.

UNCONSTITUTIONAL: OKLAHOMA'S
LOYALTY OATH [14]

In a recent decision the United States Supreme Court unanimously held the Oklahoma Loyalty Oath law unconstitutional. This statute required each state employee to take an oath that, among other things, he had not been a member during the previous five years of "any agency, party, organization, association, or group whatever which has been officially determined by the United States Attorney General or other authorized public agency of the United States to be a Communist front or subversive organization."

The case centered around the refusal of certain members of the faculty and staff of the Oklahoma Agricultural and Mechanical College to take the oath required under the act. The court found that the teachers who were discharged for refusal to comply had been deprived of their positions without due process in that the statute was arbitrary and discriminatory.

Addressing himself specifically to teachers, Justice Frankfurter in a concurring opinion stated:

> Since the affiliation which must thus be forsworn may well have been for reasons or for purposes as innocent as membership in a club of one of the established political parties, to require such an oath, on pain of a teacher's loss of his position in case of refusal to take the oath, penalizes a teacher for exercising a right of association peculiarly characteristic of our people.
>
> Such joining is an exercise of the rights of free speech and free inquiry. By limiting the power of the states to interfere with freedom of speech and freedom of inquiry and freedom of association, the Fourteenth Amendment protects all persons, no matter what their calling.

At first glance, the Oklahoma statute might not appear materially different from New York State's Feinberg Law and other loyalty legislation which the Supreme Court has upheld. However, the court found a major difference. It was that the Oklahoma statute made membership in a subversive organization grounds for automatic dismissal from state employment without trial or hearing. Moreover, the legislation did not allow for

[14] From "Oklahoma Oath Held Unconstitutional," news story. *National Education Association Journal.* 42:68. February 1953. Reprinted by permission.

the possibility that a person might have joined an organization without being aware that it was a Communist front or the possibility that the organization itself might have changed before or after he joined it.

THE LOYALTY OATH BATTLE

EDITOR'S INTRODUCTION

Loyalty oaths have been almost unanimously objected to by teachers in America's colleges and universities. Such oaths usually call for the conventional pledge of allegiance to the Constitution of the United States, of the individual state in question, and the governments thereof, but include in addition a phrase to the effect that the person taking the oath is not and has never been a member of the Communist party or any other group advocating the overthrow of the United States Government (or that of the state) by force or violence.

Such oaths are ordinarily not limited to teachers, but are asked of all public servants. Teachers, in most states, are under state civil service or similar state certification and have the status of public employees. As a result, any regulations set up to apply to public employees most generally include teachers as well.

Most of the legislation calling for teachers' loyalty oaths, however, has been intended for public school teachers in the primary and secondary schools. College teachers, unlike the public school teacher, need no special license or certificate from the state in most states. Control of the college or university, even of state schools, is in the hands of a board of regents, appointed by the state, to which is delegated complete authority over the over-all policies of the institution. Selection of faculty and the determining of their qualifications and fitness to teach are the responsibility of the colleges themselves or their administrative officers. Since the state cannot exercise direct control over the colleges, its authority can be imposed only by its control over financial support for the colleges, or over the granting of tax exemption for the college as an educational, nonprofit institution. The legislature may ask the college administration therefore to impose a loyalty oath as a condition of receiving state financial support, and the majority of loyalty oaths in colleges have thus been imposed by the college administrations, not directly by the legislature.

The loyalty oath battle in American colleges started, for all practical purposes, on the campuses of the University of California in 1949. The resulting repercussions reached from coast to coast, and 1949 is still referred to by many educators as "the year of the oath." To forestall the passage of a legislative act calling for a loyalty oath, university administrators promised legislators they would establish an oath of their own. But they didn't consult the faculty, and the resulting battle dragged on for nearly two years, with the faculty split into a number of warring factions. Numerous faculty members resigned in protest rather than take the oath before the oath was finally declared unconstitutional in the courts. In spite of the moral victory, before the court decision was announced, the state legislature passed the Levering Act, which imposed a loyalty oath on all state employees, including teachers.

Since then, teachers' professional organizations have continued to oppose the principle of a teachers' oath. The majority of the states, however, have some form of loyalty oath for public employees, including teachers, so the debate over teachers' oaths is limited primarily to the handful of states which do not yet have an oath law, or which have only a positive and not a negative oath. The positive oath is the relatively common oath of allegiance, without the affirmation that the person taking the oath is not a Communist. The swearing of non-Communist affiliation is therefore regarded by educators as a "negative" oath.

Veterans' organizations in Oregon in 1953 were persuaded to drop their proposed drive for a "negative" oath by the concerted efforts of educational groups throughout the state (see the article entitled "Oregon Legion Position" on p 120-1). Oregon already has a "positive" oath which applies to all public employees and thus to all teachers at every level (see the text of this oath on p 121).

THE FIRST BATTLE: THE UNIVERSITY OF
CALIFORNIA OATH [1]

The idea of protecting society against dangerous thoughts by the imposition of teachers' oaths is an unfortunate outcome of the jittery state of public opinion in the past two decades. The oath required of teachers in public and private institutions in Massachusetts runs as follows: "I do solemnly swear (or affirm) that I will support the Constitution of the United States and the Constitution of the Commonwealth of Massachusetts, and that I will faithfully discharge the duties of the position of . . . in . . . according to the best of my ability." Educators objected to it because they saw no reason why it should be exacted of them as a class, but it has done little harm, and presumably very little good, in the years I've watched it operate. Against Communists, it is less effective than a toy pistol. Indeed a Communist party member might get the same zest from false swearing that a Boy Scout gets from his good deed of the day. In such a group of idealistic individualists as a college faculty, however, there is always the risk that someone completely free from any suspicion of radicalism may have conscientious scruples about a required oath, and thereby be lost to the teaching profession.

A tragic illustration of this principle is afforded by the University of California, one of the greatest of our universities. Because of the eminence of its faculties, most scholars would have been inclined in 1950 to rank it in the top five American universities and some would have placed it in the top three. Very few made so great a contribution toward the winning of World War II.

Teachers at the University of California, like other public officials, take the oath provided in the state constitution in the following words: "I do solemnly swear (or affirm) that I will support the Constitution of the United States and the Constitution of the State of California, and that I will faithfully discharge the duties of my office according to the best of my ability." The state constitution provides that "no other oath, declaration, or

[1] From "Freedom in Education," by James P. Baxter, III, president, Williams College. In *Civil Liberties Under Attack*, edited by Clair Wilcox. University of Pennsylvania Press. Philadelphia. 1951. p 129-55. Reprinted by permission.

test, shall be required as a qualification for any office or public trust."

The Board of Regents adopted a resolution in October 1940 excluding members of the Communist party from employment in the University but did not proceed against any individuals under that provision. On June 24, 1949, they decided to implement their anti-Communist policy by requiring of all employees a new oath, including the words, "I am not a member of the Communist party, or under any oath, or a party to any agreement, or under any commitment that is in conflict with my obligations under this oath."

Some members of the University of California faculty were disposed to argue that since the Communist party was a legal party in California, this oath constituted a political test for membership in the faculty, and was therefore contrary to the spirit, if not the letter, of the state constitution, and that a blanket prohibition against all Communists constituted a recognition of "guilt by association." A large majority of the faculty, however, took the view that the commitments taken by all Communists deprive them of any right to a place in the company of scholars. This view was expressed in a resolution of March 7, 1950, which passed the Northern Section of the Academic Senate by a vote of 724 to 203, and the Southern Section by a vote of 301 to 65. It is important to recognize that the opponents of the new oath fully recognized that loyalty to any doctrine of totalitarianism shackles the free pursuit of truth. The March 7 resolution states this bluntly: "No person whose commitments or obligations to any organization, Communist or other, prejudice impartial scholarship and the free pursuit of truth will be employed by the university. Proved members of the Communist party, by reason of such commitments to that party, are not acceptable as members of the faculty." The faculty opponents of the new oath stressed the traditional right of teachers to be judged by their peers as to ability and integrity, and declared that once their privilege to teach became dependent on signing superimposed statements, their capacity to teach, freely and honestly, was imperiled.

The ensuing controversy attracted nation-wide attention. In April 1950, through the mediation of an alumni committee, a compromise was reached, by which every employee of the university should take the constitutional oath and then sign a letter accepting his annual appointment in which he stated, as a consideration of payment of his salary: "I am not a member of the Communist party or any other organization which advocates the overthrow of the government by force or violence, and . . . I have no commitments in conflict with my responsibilities with respect to impartial scholarship and free pursuit of truth."

The compromise provided that nonsigners might petition through the president for a hearing by the Committee on Privilege and Tenure of the Academic Senate, after which the regents would consider the findings and recommendations of the committee and the president before making a decision. Thirty-nine nonsigners, who had been cleared by this committee of any taint of communism, were appointed to their respective positions on July 21 by vote of a 10-to-9 majority of the regents, including both President Sproul and Governor Warren. At a subsequent meeting on August 25, the regents by a vote of 12 to 10, with President Sproul and Governor Warren this time in the minority, voted to rescind the appointments. The legality of this action is now being tested in the courts, but the damage to the university has reached serious proportions. . . .

According to a compilation, made recently by the faculty committee on academic freedom, the University of California has already lost 110 scholars because of the loyalty oath controversy. This number includes 26 lost through dismissal, 37 through resignation in protest against the action of the regents, and 47 through refusal of offers of appointment to the California faculty.

CALIFORNIA'S OATH FIGHT— TWO YEARS AFTERWARD [2]

The "loyalty" controversy at the University of California has been at least temporarily ended by a unanimous decision of the California Supreme Court. The court held that all state em-

[2] From "California's Loyalty Oath," editorial. New York *Times.* p E 10. October 19, 1952. Reprinted by permission.

ployees could be required to take a prescribed oath, but it also held that a special oath or declaration could not be required of college professors. The point raised by those faculty members who refused to make the required declaration was not that a professor or any other state employee had a right to belong to an organization upholding forcible overthrow of the government. It was that there should not be discrimination against professors or other teachers as such.

The soundness of this point is manifest. To ask a professor to say that he does not want to overthrow the government when other officeholders and other citizens are exempt from such a declaration is belittling and absurd. It is about the same as asking a professor, and not officeholders, to declare that he is not in favor of burning barns or robbing banks. It is like treating the high and responsible task of education as something with a criminal undertone.

Practically everyone would agree that violent revolutionists ought not to be permitted to teach in publicly supported institutions. In fact, there is no place for them in any educational institution in this country. But that never was the issue at the University of California. The issue there was whether a few self-seeking politicians could safely insult a faculty of able and honest men. It was a question of the dignity and integrity of higher education in California—and by implication elsewhere. Now it appears that a professor in California is again a first-class citizen and not under suspicion because of the nature of his occupation. In a time when so much political capital is being made by falsely accusing people of communism and other deviations this is an encouraging event.

FREEDOM AND THE LOYALTY OATH [3]

Anyone who defends traditional American liberties today is viewed with suspicion. To hold, as the Founding Fathers did, that freedom of opinion is the basis of our national life is "being soft to Communists." To plead that academic freedom is essential

[3] From "Education and the Free-Mind Principle," by A. Powell Davies, minister of All Souls' Church, Unitarian, in Washington, D.C., and one of America's best-known preachers. *New Republic*. 128:10-11. March 9, 1953. Reprinted by permission.

to the growth of healthy minds is advocating that "subversives" be protected in our schools and colleges. To believe that American ideas can stand their ground in free debate is close to treason. To be a patriot, one must assume that American principles are not defensible in open argument and that "Communist notions," unless suppressed, would prove invincible. . . .

We are forgetting what it means to be Americans. Let us be taught, then, by the Founding Fathers. By Hamilton, for instance—no liberal by temperament or in his social aims—but who was just as clear as Jefferson on what it meant to be a free American. All loyalty oaths he scornfully denounced. Such an oath, he said, "substitutes for the established and legal mode of investigating crimes and inflicting forfeitures one that is unknown to the Constitution and repugnant to the genius of our law." Among other things, he continued, such oaths "invert the order of things," obliging the citizen to establish his innocence and holding out a "bribe to perjury." . . .

It is this that our present alarmists, fearful of "subversion," seem unable to perceive. A dishonest man will take an oath of orthodoxy without the slightest scruple, having no intention of being bound by it, whereas an honest man may refuse to take it even though his views are not discordant with it, simply because it transgresses his freedom to follow his own reason and his own conscience, and thus humiliates him and makes him less a man. . . .

The loyalty oaths devised today for faculties of schools and colleges would seem to Hamilton completely useless. . . .

But besides being useless, they are pernicious. Not many teachers are injecting Communism into their teaching, "skillfully" or otherwise, because not many Communists are teachers. . . . As subverters of our educational system they are scarcely numerous enough to be a nuisance. This is so clear that it is obvious that loyalty oaths must have another purpose. Communism is a pretext: the oaths are used to make it easier to attack unpopular opinions. That is why some of our fervid and frenetic "patriots" are eager for them. They want, not so much to ferret out conspiracy, which in any case is better done by the

FBI, but to discredit freedom of discussion. They want to nullify our founding principles. Their own opinions, which they are not able to maintain by free and open debate, they wish to see imposed upon our educational system. Some of them want the educational system itself demolished; they are not aware of it—not quite, not yet—but what they would really like is a populace with education enough to maintain the mechanics of society but insufficient to encourage critical evaluation.

EDUCATORS' VIEWS ON THE OATH QUESTION [4]

Educators generally are opposed to loyalty oaths for school or college teachers. They object to being singled out as a profession, holding that by being required to declare their loyalty to this country they are placed in an inferior position. At the same time, the educational leaders of the country are opposed to the employment of any teacher who is in any way subversive or is a member of the Communist party. . . .

On the question of loyalty oaths in general, however, almost without exception the educators . . . objected to the oaths' purpose and intent.

They insisted that taking an oath would not make a teacher a better citizen; the mere signing of a paper, they said, would not change a person's viewpoint. And the educators also asserted that only a small fraction of the American teaching profession was of questionable loyalty—and that these teachers could be screened out of the classroom by other means more effective than loyalty oaths.

Dr. Ralph E. Himstead, secretary of the American Association of University Professors, said that the administration of loyalty oaths would tend to stifle the freedom of mind of many educators. Dr. Himstead declared:

Test oaths for loyalty currently required of teachers are not loyalty oaths; they are non-disloyalty oaths. They are based on a presumption of guilt, which is contrary to our law and Constitution.

[4] From "Education in Review: Supreme Court Decision Renews Controversy over Loyalty Oaths for Teachers," by Benjamin Fine, New York *Times* education editor. p E7. New York *Times*. December 21, 1952. Reprinted by permission.

The traditional American loyalty oath is an affirmative oath which pledges affirmative loyalty to the government of the United States, and is based on the presumption of innocence. Non-disloyalty oaths are alien to America and contrary to American legal and constitutional principles. I oppose non-disloyalty oaths because they are as futile as they are un-American. Estimates provided by the Federal Bureau of Investigation indicate that the number of disloyal Americans is small. The number of disloyal teachers is infinitesimally small.

Dr. Himstead said that he opposed the discriminatory application of "non-disloyalty" oaths to teachers as a class because it impairs their professional morale to the detriment of education and the general welfare. He continued:

My opposition to non-disloyalty oaths is not based on rights of teachers; it is based on the fact that such oaths create an atmosphere inimical to the freedom of the mind, an atmosphere dominated by suspicion and fear which deters forthright expression of opinion on any subject which may be regarded as controversial.

In the opinion of Dr. Katherine E. McBride, president of Bryn Mawr College, loyalty oaths are not an effective bar to the Communists. She felt that the use of these oaths might bring about the danger of limiting freedom of thought. Also, she added, the simple loyalty oath is likely to be complicated by additional provisions, such as the matter of membership in other associations, as in the Oklahoma oath. This raises the objections noted in the main opinion of the Supreme Court.

"Schools and colleges themselves are the best judges of the loyalty of their staffs," said Dr. McBride. "They should be given full responsibility and held to their responsibility for this function. Loyalty oaths are infringements of the essential rights of citizens, whether teachers or not. . . ."

Dr. David D. Henry, executive vice chancellor of New York University, declared that since subversives are not likely to hesitate to tell an untruth, loyalty oaths, in general, are an ineffectual way of dealing with disloyalty. Their only possible value, he suggested, is to lay the groundwork for perjury as a cause for dismissal. This, at its best, is an indirect way of getting at the problem, Dr. Henry said, adding:

Loyalty oaths do not harm, however, any more than do the oaths traditionally required of public officials and in many professions, if all people are treated alike. When teachers are singled out for special oaths, they should object, for such treatment is an unjustified suspicion of the profession as a whole. When teachers are treated as are all other citizens in similar employment, they should not seek to be exceptions.

According to Dr. Henry, the only effective method to maintain a teaching force of the highest standards is through employment screening, which permits the appointment only of those who meet the objectives of the profession. When employment errors are made, professional disapproval of those who do not comply can be brought into play.

Loyalty oaths are not necessary for the loyal teacher, and are ineffectual for those who are subversive, Dr. Buell G. Gallagher, president of City College, said. Dr. Gallagher declared:

> I am not in favor of compulsory loyalty oaths. They do not accomplish their ostensible purpose of keeping Communists out of the school system. The dishonest and disloyal will always swear loyalty except under certainty of conviction for perjury while the honest and loyal need no oath either to discover or to protect them.

> Loyalty oaths required of the teaching profession only are an infringement of academic rights in that they place peculiar restrictions on the profession and assume that all teachers are suspect until proved loyal. This has the effect of inhibiting the teacher from speaking his mind or joining groups on the ground that at some later date these groups might be changed in character and be declared subversive.

Declaring that no loyalty oath is needed or desired at Marquette University, the Reverend M. G. Barnett, vice president of the institution, said that "just as it expects its members who are soldiers, the Catholic Church expects its teachers to be loyal fighters for America."

"To expect a teacher to be loyal to the country that protects him and enriches his life is elementary logic," Father Barnett declared, adding: "How could such an explanation have anything to do with academic freedom to teach the truth?"

According to Dr. Richard B. Kennan, executive secretary of the National Education Association's democracy commission, teachers do not oppose affirmative loyalty oaths. They have been administered for years without protest. Teachers oppose, however, oaths that go beyond the question of loyalty to require denials of associations of prior years or that differ from oaths administered to other public employees in positions of comparable responsibility.

Oaths have proved to be ineffective as a means of discovering subversives, said Dr. Kennan. He held that the best assurances of teacher loyalty are through the careful selection of faculty members, and through the provision of adequate supervisory assistance.

LOYALTY OATHS AND THE COURTS [5]

What is there in the loyalty oaths that leads people who are themselves entirely opposed to overthrow of this government to sacrifice their livelihoods "on principle" rather than subscribe to them? Unlike the traditional oath of office to support the Constitution, which is merely a general affirmation of good intention in the performance of one's duties, the special loyalty oath expresses the suspicion that every citizen may be guilty of subversion and must clear himself. For the loyalty oath program calls upon groups of citizens en masse, without regard to the innocence or guilt of the individuals' past conduct, to prove by oath the inoffensiveness of their beliefs and associations, and to make a guarantee to the state on their political attitudes.

Logically the premise asserted by the supporters of the oath is irrefutable: certainly, anyone might be subversive. The question about the oath is whether its special contribution to the current unhealthy pitch of suspicion is justified by its benefits to security. For at the same time as the oath program teaches the rightness of universal suspicion, regardless of past acts, swearing to the oath fails to dispel suspicion because of the popular view that the disloyal would lie about their loyalty. . . .

The oath breeds excessive caution not only by intensifying the atmosphere of suspicion but also by the "pervasive threat"—as the United States Supreme Court has said with regard to censorship—once the state's power to impose a test oath is established, that the oath may be broadened in unforeseeable ways to compel an accounting for now-legitimate political and social beliefs. Indeed, besides the immediate inhibiting influence of the oaths on

[5] From "Swearing to One's Loyalty," by Nanette Dembitz, former attorney in the Department of Justice, and legal writer. *Antioch Review*, 12:195-202. Summer 1952. Reprinted by permission.

free expression, they pose a longer range danger by opening the way for the state's direction of the beliefs of the citizenry en masse on any subject on which divergence of opinion seems particularly menacing. The potentialities of state control over the individual's mind through the oath is illustrated by its initial use in Anglo-American history to search out heretical religious belief. . . .

It was out of concern for the constitutional principle that "the citizen should be secure against deprivation for past conduct . . . which was not punishable at the time it was committed," that the United States Supreme Court condemned the oath adopted by the state of Missouri in the wave of oaths following the Civil War. The post-Civil War oaths, abandoned after the court's decision, barred people from working as clergymen, lawyers, teachers, and in various other professions, or holding public offices or corporate directorships, unless they took an oath that they had given no assistance or sympathy to the Confederacy. Reminiscent of the lumping under many present-day oaths of all ex-Communists, whether or not still dangerous, the particular vice of the Missouri oath was its all-inclusiveness. In the Supreme Court's words, the Missouri oath was a harsh and unconstitutional punishment for the Confederates rather than a legitimate measure of protection, because it was "directed not merely against overt and visible acts of hostility to the government, but was intended to reach words, desires, and sympathies also" and "allowed no distinction between acts springing from malignant enmity and acts which may have been prompted by charity, or affection, or relationship."

Alexander Hamilton's fiery criticism that test oaths "hold out a bribe to perjury," quoted by a post-Civil War Supreme Court from Hamilton's attack on the oaths during the post-Revolutionary War loyalty crisis, also rings true today for a reformed ex-Communist confronted with an oath relating to his past. For if he is required in order to keep his livelihood to take an oath that he has not belonged to the party, it means that he either must perjure himself, or bar himself from employment because of a fact which he knows is no longer significant and which might never come to light. Even if the oath only requires, as some do, a disclosure as to past membership and revolutionary belief, rather than its denial, he is confronted with the choice of lying under oath or suffering the burden of a difficult and perhaps futile defense against the charge that he is still dangerous, a charge which he knows is untrue and which might never be made in the absence of his disclosure.

In the post-Civil War period the Supreme Court was more concerned with restoring the tradition of fair and equal treatment and with condemning vindictiveness than with the danger from Confederate sympathizers. Despite the greater gravity of the present Communist danger, the test oaths have such minor effectiveness in meeting it that their condemnation by thinkers of past ages still bears consideration. . . .

In the current oath wave the courts have upheld all the oaths that have been litigated, with the exception of several oaths for elective state officials which were held to conflict with the oaths provided in the state constitutions, and except for the oath adopted by the University of California Regents, which was dropped after a lower court decision against it. The courts' position has generally been that since the gravity of the Communist danger furnishes justification for an anti-Communist program, it is up to the people through the legislatures, and not the courts, to make the choice of protective measures. Thus, the Supreme Court justices have warned that the courts do not and should not determine whether the anti-Communist laws are wise or effective or whether they may not "in the long run do more harm than good." In the recent Supreme Court decision upholding New York's Feinberg Law for the discharge of "subversive" public school employees, the majority limited its consideration to the state's reasons for wanting to guard against subversion, and thought it inappropriate to evaluate either the law's effectiveness for this purpose or whether the danger was great enough to justify the evils of the surveillance system the law creates. It is therefore a misplaced confidence, as the justices have pointed out, for the citizen to trust that a law will be held unconstitutional merely because it is undesirable, and to fail on this assumption to make up his own mind on its merits. . . .

The important issue is whether the effectiveness of the oaths to secure loyalty is sufficient to outweigh the harm they do by

generating fear and overcaution. . . . It is true that the current
loyalty oaths do not suppress free expression by directly outlaw-
ing any socially useful belief, expression, or association. But the
benefits of free expression are as much lost when it is sacrificed
through fear as when it is arrested by outright suppression. And
if through disuse the custom of freedom is lost, there is little
hope of sustaining the love of freedom and the will to resist its
suppression.

AAUP OPPOSITION TO
LOYALTY OATH · REQUIREMENTS [6]

A teacher who misuses his classroom or other relationships
with his students for propaganda purposes or for the advocacy
of legally defined subversive action, or who in his extramural
relationships is guilty of a legally defined subversive act, is
responsible as an individual for the violation of professional
principles or of the law of the land, as the case may be. Such
a teacher should be dismissed, provided his guilt is established
by evidence adduced in a proceeding in which he is given a full
measure of due process, as due process is understood in American
constitutional law.

The reaffirmation of these views is made with full awareness that in recent years state legislation has gone far in impos-
ing non-disloyalty test oaths upon teachers in the public schools
and in the publicly controlled colleges and universities; that the
tendency in legislation has been strong to disqualify persons
from teaching because of their past or present organizational
affiliations; and that the Supreme Court of the United States has
sustained the constitutionality of such legislation. Yet the
Supreme Court, although it has affirmed the powers of legislatures to determine factors relevant to the fitness of teachers in
publicly controlled institutions, has withheld approval of any
action which makes membership in a lawful organization, in and
of itself, ground for disqualification. Thus, in the Oklahoma
Loyalty Oath Case, the Supreme Court of the United States in a

[6] From resolution adopted by the American Association of University Professors
at its 39th Annual Meeting in Chicago, March 27-28, 1953. *American Association
of University Professors Bulletin.* 39:91-93. Spring 1953. Reprinted by permission.
(Passages of the statement dealing with other aspects of academic freedom are reprinted on p 64-5 and p 138-9 of this book.)

unanimous decision on December 12, 1952, declared unconstitutional such an act of the legislature of Oklahoma.

The case against non-disloyalty test oaths was well stated in the concurring opinion of Mr. Justice Black . . . :

> The Oklahoma Oath Statute is but one manifestation of a national network of laws aimed at coercing and controlling the minds of men. Test oaths are notorious tools of tyranny. When used to shackle the minds they are, or at least they should be, unspeakably odious to a free people. Test oaths are made still more dangerous when combined with bills of attainder which like this Oklahoma Statute impose pains and penalties for past lawful associations and utterances.
>
> Governments need and have ample power to punish treasonable acts, but it does not follow that they must have a further power to punish thought and speech as distinguished from acts. . . . And I cannot too often repeat my belief that the right to speak on matters of public concern must be wholly free or eventually be wholly lost.

Experience has abundantly demonstrated that neither the organizational affiliations of a teacher, if lawful, nor his social, economic, political or religious opinions, however difficult for others to understand and however distasteful to others they may be, are sufficient evidence of disqualification for work in the academic profession. The acceptance of the contrary view leads logically to and invites non-disloyalty test oaths for teachers, and inquisitions into their beliefs and associations and into the internal affairs and policies of colleges and universities. Such oaths and inquisitions are inimical to these institutions and the American way of life. Unprofessional conduct or unlawful acts of a kind that might disqualify one for academic work are personal and can be dealt with wisely and justly only in a proceeding directed to the individual.

OREGON LEGION POSITION [7]

There is, at present, considerable discussion in the state concerning the teachers' loyalty oath. We, of the American Legion, concur in the stand taken on January 3, 1953, by the legislative committee of the veterans' organizations in the state of Oregon . . . not to ask the legislature for any additional loyalty

[7] From statement of Karl L. Wagner, State Commander of the American Legion in Oregon. Undated press release. The American Legion. Department of Oregon. 702 General George A. White Building, Portland 4, Oregon.

oaths. It appears that the existing affirmative loyalty oaths now on the statute books are sufficient, if enforced by school authorities.

The committee further believes that the school officials and the Board of Education should be fully qualified and should have the opportunity, if it is necessary, to clean their own house without being harassed by outside organizations. . . .

The committee takes the position that sincere educators and public officials are best qualified to enforce loyalty laws. The committee realizes that an educator must, to be effective, be allowed academic freedom, but emphasizes that such freedom does not extend to the privilege of teaching precepts that are inimicable to our system of government.

OREGON'S "POSITIVE" OATH [8]

OREGON STATE SYSTEM OF HIGHER EDUCATION
Oath or Affirmation of Allegiance
(As required in Chapter 115, Laws of Oregon 1921)

"I solemnly swear, or affirm, that I will support the constitution of the State of Oregon and the laws enacted thereunder, and that I will teach, by precept and example, respect for the flags of the United States and of the State of Oregon; reverence for law and order and individual allegiance to the government of our country, the United States of America."

....
Name
....
Rank or Title
....
Institution

Subscribed and sworn to before me

this..........day of.............................A.D.19......

....
Notary Public

My commission expires...................................
NOTARIAL
SEAL

[8] Oath, required under Chapter 115, Laws of Oregon 1921, to be taken by all teachers in public, private and parochial schools or other institutions of learning.

THE FIFTH AMENDMENT CONTROVERSY

EDITOR'S INTRODUCTION

One of the most significant developments in the conflict between academic freedom and loyalty has been the growing concern over the rights of witnesses before congressional committees. The educators called before the Jenner and Velde committees to answer questions as to present or past membership in the Communist party have, in the majority of instances, relied upon the protection of the Fifth Amendment in refusing to offer any testimony relating to political affiliations. Following such refusals, on the part of certain of their faculty members, a number of universities have conducted inquiries into the fitness of the individuals in question to remain on the faculty. Quite often, the college or university has demanded the resignation of the faculty member. In certain other instances, the school administration has issued a public statement to the effect that refusal to testify before a congressional (or any other legislative) committee is grounds for automatic dismissal without further inquiry and without appeal. This procedure has been legalized under New York's Feinberg Law, and generally represents the viewpoint expressed by the Association of American Universities, and by college alumni throughout the nation.

The basic issue of the Fifth Amendment controversy is whether a college or university can morally and ethically dismiss a member of its faculty who makes use of the Fifth Amendment to protect himself from self-incrimination. It is assumed, naturally, that he genuinely believes it necessary to take such action, and that he is not merely expressing defiance or disapproval. The situation is somewhat further complicated by the determination of college administrations to run their own affairs without dictation from outside groups, especially legislatures. In consequence, while there have been almost unanimous expressions by college administrators that the Communist teacher has no place in teaching, and that they would fire any present member of the Communist party they might discover, still they cling to the "right" to hire or retain whomever they please. The dilemma of the college administrator in trying to uphold this principle in face of strong public pressure to "get rid of the Communists" probably accounts for the recent demand that faculty members called before congressional committees "co-operate" in the future.

Faced by the multiple pressures of public opinion, the press, the regents and alumni, plus the negative effect created by the lengthy procession of Fifth Amendment witnesses, the school administrator's first concern will naturally be to protect the good name of his institution. At the same time, as an educator, loyal to the guiding principle of academic freedom, he attempts to provide the procedural protection necessary to the individual faculty member under the tenure system. During the past year a number of major institutions have faced the problem, and each has attempted to solve it in its own way. Harvard refused to fire the faculty members who resorted to the Fifth Amendment defense, but placed them "on probation." Rutgers was first to dismiss a professor for refusing to testify. At other universities, actions ranged from public defense of the faculty member and his retention to summary dismissal on grounds of insubordination and a variety of other charges. One such case, that of Professor Darling at Ohio State, is detailed briefly on p 145-51.

The problem of the Fifth Amendment witness is undeniably a difficult one for the colleges. The issue is simply what to do with him. Defending him or taking no action may subject the university to serious charges that it shelters and encourages subversive teachers, and tends to throw suspicion on all other members of the faculty. Has the professor in question any reasonable claim to rights or privileges which might so endanger his institution or his colleagues? On the other hand, isn't the institution effectively denying the principle of academic freedom, and of tenure, which have been established, more or less securely, over a forty-year period? Does the university have the right to destroy a teacher's professional career, labeling him disloyal in effect, when his only apparent offense is the exercise of a constitutional right guaranteed all citizens in a democratic society? These are some of the questions at issue in the controversy over the exercise of the Fifth Amendment by witnesses before legislative investigating committees.

HARVARD CRIMSON REPORT ON FIFTH AMENDMENT ISSUE [1]

By June 1 of this year, over a hundred university teachers had declined to answer questions posed by three congressional committees on grounds of the Fifth Amendment to the Constitution of the United States. Fifty-four had been dismissed or suspended from their jobs. Others were on probation or under official censure. All, according to polls of public opinion, had received the tacit condemnation of their fellow citizens.

Leading the investigations were the Senate Internal Security Subcommittee . . . and the House Un-American Activities Committee. . . . In almost every state in the union, state legislative committees had started or were preparing similar investigations.

Faced with this onslaught, both professors and governing boards of the nation's universities faced the problem of proper use of the Fifth Amendment, which had become the only legal defense against the committee's questions.

Many considered it a moral issue, and believed any testimony inferred their sanction to the committee's proceedings. Some felt that they had a perfect legal right to remain silent, for if they once spoke witnesses would be produced by the committees to corner them on grounds of perjury. Even among the foremost legal minds in the nation there was no agreement. Morris L. Ernst . . . wrote the following to the *Crimson*:

> By and large, a human being only tells on those who violate the folkways of his own group.
>
> This is the essence of the dilemma under the Fifth Amendment. Outside of a few people, often represented by attorneys following the Communist line, I suggest that practically all of the people who pleaded the Fifth Amendment were willing to tell everything they knew about

[1] From "Education and the Fifth Amendment," news story. *Harvard Crimson,* Fifth Annual Academic Freedom Report. p 1. June 10, 1953. Reprinted by permission.

the Communist membership except that they had an understandable reluctance to tell on those people who had gotten out of the movement and were leading unmolested, decent, pro-democracy lives. We have taught our children not to be tattle-tales, but now we are putting on a public parade of witnesses to testify against their upbringing. . . .

Traveling from city to city the investigators followed a hit-and-run tactic that made it difficult for universities to formulate any unified policy on what to do with professors who used the Fifth Amendment. In the initial confusion of November through January, some schools immediately suspended such teachers, others judged each case on its own merits. Not until March 24 were the thirty-four universities of the country who form the American Association of Universities able to agree on a single policy statement. This statement denied the privilege of tenure to Communist party members and said the use of the Fifth Amendment by a teacher means "he must bear a heavy burden of proof as to his fitness to continue teaching." The AAU's legal interpretation of the Fifth Amendment followed pretty much the view first clarified by two Harvard Law School professors in a letter to the *Crimson* on January 13. Zechariah Chafee, Jr. and Arthur E. Sutherland said:

The underlying principle to remember in considering the subject is the duty of the citizen to cooperate in government. He has no option to say, "I do not approve of this Grand Jury or that congressional committee; I dislike its members and its objectives; therefore I will not tell it what I know." He is neither wise nor legally justified in attempting political protest by standing silent when obligated to speak. The citizen is ordinarily required, when summoned, to give testimony to a court, legislative committee or other body vested with subpoena power and if he refuses to do so he is punishable. Subpoena power has proved necessary to the conduct of government: it is the correlative of the guarantee to an accused in the Sixth Amendment that he shall "have compulsory process for obtaining witnesses in his favor."

To this general duty of the citizen the privilege against self-incrimination is an extraordinary exception. The Federal Constitution prohibits all Federal officers from requiring anyone to give testimony tending to prove that he is guilty of a crime. . . .

There are several current misconceptions about the testimonial privilege to remain silent. The witness is not the ultimate judge of the tendency of an answer to incriminate him. . . .

Mere embarrassment is not an excuse: the witness must be subjecting himself to some degree of danger of conviction of a criminal offense. . . . A sense of sportsmanship toward suspected associates is not an excuse: the Fifth Amendment grants no privilege to protect one's friends. If a man feels that he has a personal code compelling this reticence, he must pay for his scruple by standing the punishment society prescribes.

Difficult questions arise when a witness is asked if he now is or ever has been a member of the Communist party. The Internal Security Act of 1950 provides "Neither the holding of office nor membership in any Communist organization by any person shall constitute per se a violation of . . . this section or of any other criminal statute." Whether this refers only to Federal statutes or was intended to include state statutes as well is not clear, but the section tends to militate against immunity when the question is asked with reference to a Federal offense. Certainly the fact that disclosure of present or past association with the Communist party will cause trouble for the witness with his church, his lodge, his union, his employer, or his university, does not excuse him from answering questions about it when subpoenaed before a competent body. . . .

A privileged refusal to testify is not an admission of guilt for the purposes of criminal prosecution. Its effect on popular opinion is, of course, not within constitutional control. A refusal may mean only that the witness has innocently got into a situation where he is apparently though not actually guilty of a crime; but fairly or not, the fact that he feels it necessary to refuse information to a government agency on the ground that it will tend to incriminate him inevitably casts a shadow on his reputation. . . .

There were universities like Rutgers which used the Chafee-Sutherland thesis to justify immediate dismissal. Harvard, in its dealings with professors who used the constitutional privilege, seemed to agree in theory, but the Harvard Corporation adopted a policy of judging each case on its own qualifications, and it was not until May 20 that it issued a statement on Associate Professor of Physics Wendell H. Furry who had first used the amendment before Velde's committee on February 25.

We deplore the use of the Fifth Amendment by a member of our faculty [wrote the Harvard Corporation].

In the first place we think full and candid testimony by all teachers would disclose that there is little Communist activity today in educational institutions. But more important, the use of the Fifth Amendment is in our view entirely inconsistent with the candor to be expected of one devoted to the pursuit of truth. It is no excuse that the primary purpose of its use is to protect one's friends, or to express one's feelings that congressional committees are by-passing the constitutional safeguards of due process of law, or to avert a danger of prosecution for perjury in case one's testimony should later be contradicted by the false testimony of others. Furthermore, since we are not conducting a criminal trial, we will not shut our eyes to the inference of guilt which the use of the Fifth Amendment creates as a matter of common sense. Hence, the use of the Fifth Amendment by a member of our teaching staff within the critical field of his possible domination by the Communist party, makes it necessary in our judgment for us to inquire into the full facts. . . .

For it is obvious, although all responsible groups have agreed that the investigations themselves have done more harm than good to American universities, that the use of the Fifth Amendment is food for sensational journalism, which damns an instructor's university as well as the man himself. In Furry's testimony, for an instance, the physics professor stated that he felt the committee had no right to inquire into his beliefs. Yet, he was willing to go into detail about his views against fascism. The tremendous concern with academic freedom as an abstract doctrine often caused men to tacitly implicate a university in their refusal to answer questions. . . .

There was yet another view, however, which enabled a witness to hold his moral convictions about incriminating others without using the Fifth Amendment. First used before the Jenner Committee by Irving Goldman, who teaches anthropology at Sarah Lawrence College, it can best be called "calculated contempt." To Goldman and his counsel, Arthur Garfield Hays, the best way to reconcile one's conscience without harming his college was speaking openly about personal activities, refusing to testify about others.

Goldman admitted he was a member of the Communist party, which he left in 1942. He would not answer any questions about his associates, not on grounds of the Fifth Amendment, but purely on moral grounds. The trustees of Sarah Lawrence backed Goldman, while the Jenner Committee failed to even cite him for contempt. . . .

We must conclude that complete silence is not the answer for those who testify. There are, of course, some cases in which use of the Fifth Amendment may be applicable. But in the great majority it has not helped either the universities or the professors who have used it.

OBLIGATIONS OF UNIVERSITY FACULTIES—
AAU STATEMENT [2]

In the eyes of the law, the university scholar has no more and no less freedom than his fellow citizens outside a university. None the less, because of the vital importance of the university to civilization, membership in its society of scholars enhances the prestige of persons admitted to its fellowship after probation and upon the basis of achievement in research and teaching. The university supplies a distinctive forum and, in so doing, strengthens the scholar's voice. When his opinions challenge existing orthodox points of view, his freedom may be more in need of defense than that of men in other professions. The guarantee of tenure to professors of mature and proven scholarship is one such defense. As in the case of judges, tenure protects the scholar against undue economic or political pressures and ensures the continuity of the scholarly process.

There is a line at which "freedom" or "privilege" begins to be qualified by legal "duty" and "obligation." The determination of the line is the function of the legislature and the courts. The ultimate interpretation and application of the First and Fourteenth Amendments are the function of the United States Supreme Court; but every public official is bound by his oath of office to respect and preserve the liberties guaranteed therein. These are not to be determined arbitrarily or by public outcry. The line thus drawn can be changed by legislative and judicial action; it has varied in the past because of prevailing anxieties as well as by reason of "clear and present" danger. Its location is subject to, and should receive, criticism, both popular and judicial. However

[2] From "The Rights and Responsibilities of Universities and Their Faculties," policy statement of the Association of American Universities (AAU), March 30, 1953. (Reprinted in *United States News & World Report*. 34:65-7. April 10, 1953; also New York *Times*. p 12. March 31, 1953. Passages of the statement dealing with other aspects of academic freedom are reprinted on p 162-5 of this book.)

much the location of the line may be criticized, it cannot be disregarded with impunity. Any member of a university who crosses the duly established line is not excused by the fact that be believes the line ill-drawn. When the speech, writing, or other actions of a member of a faculty exceed lawful limits, he is subject to the same penalties as other persons. In addition, he may lose his university status.

Historically the word "university" is a guarantee of standards. It implies endorsement not of its members' views but of their capability and integrity. Every scholar has an obligation to maintain this reputation. By ill-advised, though not illegal, public acts or utterances he may do serious harm to his profession, his university, to education and to the general welfare. He bears a heavy responsibility to weigh the soundness of his opinions and the manner in which they are expressed. His effectiveness, both as scholar and teacher, is not reduced but enhanced if he has the humility and the wisdom to recognize the fallibility of his own judgment. He should remember that he is as much a layman as anyone else in all fields except those in which he has special competence. Others, both within and without the university, are as free to criticize his opinions as he is free to express them; "academic freedom" does not include freedom from criticism.

As in all acts of association, the professor accepts conventions which become morally binding Above all, he owes his colleagues in the university complete candor and perfect integrity, precluding any kind of clandestine or conspiratorial activities. He owes equal candor to the public. If he is called upon to answer for his convictions, it is his duty as a citizen to speak out. It is even more definitely his duty as a professor. Refusal to do so, on whatever legal grounds, cannot fail to reflect upon a profession that claims for itself the fullest freedom to speak and the maximum protection of that freedom available in our society. In this respect, invocation of the Fifth Amendment places upon a professor a heavy burden of proof of his fitness to hold a teaching position and lays upon his university an obligation to re-examine his qualifications for membership in its society.

In all universities faculties exercise wide authority in internal affairs. The greater their autonomy, the greater their share of responsibility to the public. They must maintain the highest standards and exercise the utmost wisdom in appointments and promotions. They must accept their share of responsibility for the discipline of those who fall short in the discharge of their academic trust.

The universities owe their existence to legislative acts and public charters. A state university exists by constitutional and legislative acts, an endowed university enjoys its independence by franchise from the state and by custom. The state university is supported by public funds. The endowed university is benefited by tax exemptions. Such benefits are conferred upon the universities not as favors, but in furtherance of the public interest. They carry with them public obligation of direct concern to the faculties of the universities as well as to the governing boards.

Legislative bodies from time to time may scrutinize these benefits and privileges. It is clearly the duty of universities and their members to cooperate in official inquiries directed to those ends. When the powers of legislative inquiry are abused, the remedy does not lie in non-cooperation or defiance; it is to be sought through the normal channels of informed public opinion.

THE WITNESSES AND THEIR ALTERNATIVES [3]

What sort of person would feel any conflict of alternatives if he should be called before an investigating committee?

First . . . there are the former Communists. . . . The former Communist begins the problem of silence . . . with concerns of self-protection. . . .

A second witness who may be tempted to remain silent is the united-fronter, who may be neither a Communist nor a member of an organization listed as subversive by the United States Attorney General, but who is active in organizations which share some political premises with the Communists. . . . For the united-fronter . . . silence serves for political protest and self-protection. . . .

[3] From "Do Silent Witnesses Defend Civil Liberties?" by Alan F. Westin, graduate of the Harvard Law School and member of the District of Columbia bar. *Commentary.* 15:537-46. June 1953. Reprinted by permission.

Most committees investigating subversion have been calling as witnesses persons who are known, on credible evidence, to be Communist party members or former Communists, with only an occasional united-fronter being summoned. Yet, if we are to be logically complete, there is a third type of possible silent witness to consider. This is the liberal, a man with neither Communist nor united-front affiliations, but one who views the investigations as threatening *his* ideas and *his* values. This man fears that the march of investigating committees through such nongovernmental areas as labor unions, public schools, and cultural media has already created, in Justice William O. Douglas's phrase, "a black silence of fear" in the nation. . . . He feels that committee plans to probe into universities, churches, law, medicine, and journalism will only create a dangerous and distorted picture in the public mind.

Faced by this prospect, our hypothetical liberal may feel that it is time for men of courage to be conscientious objectors. . . .

What is the constitutional and political setting in which they must resolve their dilemma? There are four "ground rules" in 1953, and they can be summarized as follows:

(1) . . . Congress may now investigate any subject which (a) provides information as a basis for legislation or (b) establishes that no legislation is needed; and a congressional committee may compel testimony as long as its questions are "pertinent to the inquiry." (Under Title 2, Section 192 of the United States Code, a witness who refuses to answer pertinent questions is liable to a $1,000 fine and one year in prison.)

(2) The Supreme Court has not decided, one way or the other, whether the free speech, free press, and free assembly guarantees of the First Amendment place any limit upon the scope of congressional investigations, or insure any right to privacy for political associations. (Lower Federal courts have ruled that it does not.) In 1949 and again in 1953, the Supreme Court was presented with appeals in which this question was involved, but . . . the justices declined to rule on the First Amendment issue.

(3) The Fifth Amendment, providing in part that "no witness . . . shall be compelled in any criminal case to be a witness

against himself," does give a citizen the privilege of refusing to answer questions before a court, grand jury, or legislative committee where his answer might put him in jeopardy of legal penalties. This jeopardy must be of criminal punishment or forfeitures, however, and fear of damages to reputation or loss of employment have not been held to be within the protection of the amendment. . . .

In 1950, the Supreme Court ruled that a witness who properly invoked the Fifth Amendment could not be required to answer questions relating to Communist party activities (*Blau* versus *United States*). Such answers, the Court declared, might tend to furnish "a link in the chain of evidence" leading to prosecution under the Smith Act, which forbids conspiracy to advocate the overthrow of the government by force. After the Blau decision, fifty-nine witnesses who had been indicted for contempt of Congress were released by Federal decisions, all of which upheld a right to silence under the Fifth Amendment. In the past few years, hundreds of witnesses have claimed the protection of the Fifth Amendment, and committees now accept the claim as a valid ground for refusing to testify.

(4) Although witnesses who have properly invoked the Fifth Amendment before congressional committees have not been convicted for contempt, official and unofficial reprisals have come to follow almost automatically upon the claim of such a privilege. The public—rightly or wrongly—has viewed the claim of Fifth Amendment shelter as an admission of at least near-guilt. This has led to firings in the cases of United Nations employees, New York and Boston school teachers, movie and radio personnel, and college professors from a host of institutions. . . . A special committee of the American Bar Association has put forth a proposal that any attorney who claims the Fifth Amendment be disbarred.

Given this setting, the years since . . . 1947 have produced three hypothetical alternatives which a "hostile" witness could choose to follow. . . .

The first alternative maintains that the privilege against self-incrimination should be used to register opposition to "McCarthyism" and to safeguard lawful but unpopular political activi-

ties. . . . In the seventeenth century, the English courts of Star
Chamber and High Commission attempted to extract confessions
of heresy and sedition from religious dissenters. From the opposition of Puritans, common law lawyers, and parliamentary
supporters to these royal courts of inquisition came the British
privilege against self-incrimination. This heritage from the
mother country . . . led virtually all of the thirteen colonies, and
later the Federal Bill of Rights, to include a provision against
compulsory testimony.

Citing this history of the privilege as a weapon for religious
and political liberty, and a guarantee against brutal or unfair
treatment, the Fifth Amendment advocate urges that a man
whose affiliations might endanger him—the Communist, the
former Communist, or the united-fronter—should protect himself as the Constitution permits, especially since he prevents by
his conduct any "inquiries into political belief" by congressional
investigators. . . .

The second major position maintains that . . . this Fifth
Amendment line of conduct . . . has become ineffective as a
means by which non-Communists can register any opinions before senators, school authorities, or the public. . . .

When a witness uses the Fifth Amendment to avoid the
"$64.00 question," the average newspaper reader assumes that
the witness is a Communist. . . .

This position . . . argues that one should be silent, not by
claiming the Fifth Amendment but by invoking the First
Amendment. The defender of civil liberties should express opposition to investigations of political loyalty as distinguished
from unlawful acts, and should assert that our rights as citizens
to free speech, press, and assembly prohibit such inquiries. One
who adheres to this view recognizes that it would entail a citation for contempt, since the First Amendment gives no constitutional right to silence under current constitutional decisions. But
this citation would put before the Supreme Court once more its
refusal to rule whether there are in fact any First Amendment
bounds to congressional hearings. . . .

The third policy we have to consider would have a witness
claim neither the Fifth nor the First Amendments, but would

insist upon a "clean hands" doctrine as the only choice worth the consideration of the non-Communist who seeks to preserve our climate of political freedom. . . . The clean-hands proponent argues, the cause of freedom is best served not by silence but by free *speech*. Witnesses should answer the questions about their organizational memberships or actions, and then defend their current political positions before the committee and thus before public opinion. . . . In addition, open witnesses could strike a meaningful blow on behalf of their profession or institution which a policy of silence makes impossible. . . .

So, advises the clean-hands advocate, the former Communist should admit his earlier associations, the united-fronter should openly fight for the views he holds, and the liberal should tread that gray path which has been his route ever since he renounced simple black-and-white.

The first position, that of invoking the Fifth Amendment, has been the one utilized by the overwhelming number of witnesses called before committee investigators. In the hearings on communism in education held before the Subcommittee on Internal Security (Senator Jenner), forty-five witnesses from twelve different universities have (up to this writing) invoked the privilege against self-incrimination at public sessions, and many times that number did so in closed, executive proceedings of that committee. The transcripts suggest that most of these witnesses were Communists or former Communists. To my knowledge, no one except Professor Barrows Dunham of Temple University has attempted First Amendment silence since the United States Court of Appeals . . . rejected the First Amendment as a constitutional ground for silence. Quite a number of witnesses have chosen the third position—in education, for example, professors from Smith College, Massachusetts Institute of Technology, Sarah Lawrence, and other institutions. No witness has yet admitted that he is a Communist at the present time, and tried to defend that position.

I have dubbed the clean-hands approach "profoundest wisdom" for the non-Communist, and it is necessary to defend that designation. We must begin, in considering this matter, by realizing that our major goal in defending freedom is not (or not only) a proper Supreme Court decision, but rather an atmosphere free of that public-imposed orthodoxy which, a hundred years ago, John Stuart Mill observed to be the real threat to liberty. No one argues against the right of Greasy-Thumb Guzik or Gerald L. K. Smith to have their sentences for contempt of Congress reversed by the Supreme Court; at the same time, most citizens do not rush forward to help these defendants into teaching posts or screen-writing jobs. As long as witnesses employ the tactics of silence rather than of defending what they believe, and their right to believe it, they will receive only that toleration which society and the Constitution reserve for the mobster or the racist—no more, no less. Witnesses who would be evaluated on a different basis must be willing to demonstrate by open speech that they are political dissenters, not conspirators. . . .

Of course, the central difficulty felt by many who would otherwise accept the clean-hands position is that it would probably require former Communists employing it to answer questions as to their associates. The law seems to be that once a witness testifies as to his own membership, he has waived the Fifth Amendment privilege (having "incriminated" himself) and cannot use it later to close off questions about persons he knew or knows. . . .

A more appealing solution would be for a witness to answer questions about himself while refusing, without any Fifth Amendment claim, to name his associates. . . . A witness . . . , while risking contempt citation, would not be creating the aura of *personal* conspiracy which attends the refusal to answer on the Fifth Amendment. To date, only two witnesses have chosen this line. . . .

Despite the initial attraction of this position, I would suggest that complete responsiveness is still the wiser choice. First of all, a former Communist should think twice before reserving to himself the decision as to whether his former comrades are *presently* dangerous to American society. As a former Communist, he knows at first hand that the devotion and discipline of the average party member makes him an instrument of party policy, and that this degree of commitment makes the Communist capable of executing directives which could jeopardize civil liberties and the national security. If the witness's associates have also left the party, they can say so; if they have not, then the former Communist must weigh the personal code of honor against the need for full disclosure in a free society under attack.

Second, if the witness elects partial (or complete) silence on the theory that this prevents him from being "smeared" or "black-listed," he is in effect choosing to parallel the Communist strategy, which wants all witnesses to choose silence in order to camouflage the activities of Communist party members. . . . Recourse to the First or Fifth Amendments leaving unexplained the evidence of committee counsel will be very costly to the ex-party member, whereas open speech and sincere explanation of his change in loyalty would be accepted by most of the nation. . . .

Liberty has only rarely been defended by silence. In this country, at this time, I think it must be defended by speaking out.

THE OBLIGATION TO TESTIFY [4]

Should one who is called before . . . a committee testify about his present and past membership and activities in the Communist party? Should a witness give the names of persons whom he knew to be engaged in such activities? In my opinion the answer to both these questions is "yes," though the methods of the committee chairmen make it difficult to adhere to one of the first principles of democracy.

We need to be quite clear about the point under discussion. It is not sufficient to challenge the competence of the committees, or even their procedures. These committees have not always deserved respect and have often merited contempt, but they were established by overwhelming majorities of Congress and have strong support in public opinion. It is an essential precept of popular government that the citizen must cooperate with its agencies, even though he disapproves of their objectives, criticizes them, and seeks to bring about a change. Democratic government cannot long endure if each citizen may decide for himself when he will submit and when he will refuse. . . .

[4] From "Should Teachers Testify?" guest editorial, by Benjamin F. Wright, president, Smith College. *Saturday Review*. p22-3. September 26, 1953. Reprinted by permission.

To the best of my knowledge and belief there is no real danger from communism in the colleges and universities of this country at the present time. During the thirties a handful of teachers and students accepted the Communist party as the only available means to fight unemployment and fascism. The fifties are quite different from the thirties, partly because of the defeat of fascism in the war, partly because the depression with its tremendous unemployment is gone, partly because of Korea and a general awareness of the nature and objectives of communism. Marxism has virtually no appeal for the students of today. But the very fact that a number of witnesses have refused to give testimony, either about themselves or about others, has obscured the present situation. Many people believe that there must be a present conspiracy when witness after witness refuses to testify on the ground that an answer would tend to incriminate. Some of the latter are presumably guilty, others profess to think of themselves as innocent martyrs to the principles of free thought and association. What right they have to be included in that frequently honorable, and sometimes noble, category remains unclear. And certainly they have involved the academic profession, as well as themselves, in an atmosphere of suspicion.

One of the reasons most frequently given by teachers for believing that those called before congressional committees should not testify is that the committees have no right to investigate political opinions. When opinion alone is involved that view cannot be disagreed with. . . . But the Communist party is not just a political organization. It is also conspiratorial. Academic freedom, like freedom of speech, does not include the right to engage in conspiracy, whether Communist, Fascist, or one involving a breach of the ordinary criminal laws. If there are persons in the academic profession engaged in such conspiracies we should know about them. The colleges must have, and protect, the critical minds, but they are not sanctuaries for those who would follow the example of Klaus Fuchs.

It is a necessary corollary of academic freedom that every teacher disclose the affiliations which predetermine his conclusions and actions. The Communist is not a free man as we have understood that term, and he is prohibited by the nature of his controlling faith from following wherever the argument or the research leads, just as he is rendered incapable of giving an objective judgment on virtually all controversial issues.

No sensitive and conscientious person would be other than distressed by the necessity of identifying those whom he had known at one time as members of the Communist party. But does not the moral basis of democratic government, the doctrine which in the eighteenth century was known as the social contract —the agreement of each with all to cooperate in establishing a commonwealth—require that such testimony be given about others as well as about oneself? If a former member of the Communist party is now opposed to communism how can he reconcile his opposition with refusal to disclose the names of those known to him to have been Communists at one time? He may believe that they are no longer members but he can never be sure that that is a fact. Deceit and dissimulation are the policies of that organization. It is difficult to see how the citizen who believes in democratic institutions can reconcile the refusal to give information with the responsibilities of citizenship in a free society, how the teacher can reconcile that attitude with respect for the candid and open statement of the truth which is an essential element of academic freedom. Nor can they ignore the effect upon public sentiment. Though the justification for the investigation of communism in schools and colleges almost certainly came to an end some years ago, if it ever existed, refusal to answer on grounds of self-incrimination so obscures the present situation that many citizens and members of Congress continue to believe that a conspiracy exists which warrants investigation.

AAUP RESOLUTION [5]

If in the investigation of members of faculties of institutions of higher education by a committee of the Congress of the United States or other legislative bodies, a faculty member invokes the Fifth Amendment of the Constitution of the United

[5] From resolution adopted by the American Association of University Professors at its 39th Annual Meeting in Chicago, March 27-28, 1953. *American Association of University Professors Bulletin.* 39:95-6. Spring 1953. Reprinted by permission. (Passages of the statement dealing with other aspects of academic freedom are reprinted on p 64-5 and p 119-20 of this book.)

States as the reason for not replying to questions of the Committee concerning his views and affiliations . . . invoking the Fifth Amendment in these circumstances is not, in and of itself, justifiable cause for the dismissal of the faculty member. However, since a decision to invoke the Fifth Amendment involves complex legal and ethical considerations, this statement is not to be construed as advising or generally approving such action by teachers under investigation.

THE ISSUES IN THE FIFTH AMENDMENT CONTROVERSY [6]

The general principle of academic freedom has been sufficiently expounded, though it is as yet by no means understood by the general public. The more immediate question is the relation of this principle to the congressional committees of investigation. This question is confused by the fact that it involves three different questions:

1. Is it desirable that these committees should investigate higher education? There is little doubt of the constitutionality of such investigations, but in view of their demagogic motivation, loose methods, vindictive tone, and the general effect of terror there can be no doubt that, however constitutional, they should not be "welcomed." . . .

2. Should a college or university dismiss a teacher automatically, on the sole ground of his invoking his constitutional rights to justify refusal to testify before such committees? The answer is "No." By so doing, the institutions virtually turn over to government their authority to hire and fire. A refusal to testify does not constitute sufficient evidence for dismissal, even when it constitutes sufficient evidence for the charge of contempt. The institution will take account of other considerations, and reach its own decision, on educational grounds.

There is no reason why the institution should serve as the executioner—the instrument by which to penalize those who have offended the committees, or against whom the committees

[6] From "Issues in College Inquiries," letter to the New York *Times* by Ralph Barton Perry, philosopher and author, professor of philosophy, Harvard University. New York *Times.* p 26. April 28, 1953. Reprinted by permission.

have obtained what they consider to be unfavorable evidence. Even when individuals have been convicted of a crime, or have given offense to public sentiment, the institution has itself to decide, in each individual case, whether such legal guilt or public condemnation disqualifies him from serving the institution. The institution should reserve its own judgment, and arrive at it on its own grounds and by its own forms of due process.

It is the university, be it noted, that has entered into a contractual engagement with its teachers and has extended to them the privileges of tenure. The issue here is the autonomy of the educational institution as regards the employment of its own staff. It has a duty to resist all "pressures," whether they come from congressional committees or from public clamor or from its own alumni.

To this question is related the question whether a teacher should be dismissed on the ground that a committee has found him to be a Communist, or member of a group which the committee considers to be communistic or communistical, or has found him to be a member of an organization on the Attorney General's famous list. There are two possibilities: such membership may be illegal or legal. If it is illegal it is for the courts to convict and fix the penalty; the institution has no obligation to apply the additional penalty of dismissal. If it is legal, and there is no judicial punishment, the institution is under no obligation to create a penalty.

This, of course, does not mean that such membership, whether legal or illegal, may not be taken into consideration by the institution in its own determination of the individual's academic rights and usefulness. If the institution decides, all things considered, that the individual has a "closed mind," or is a mere puppet, or is promoting subversiveness, or is neglecting his work through preoccupation with his party activities, it will and should give weight to these considerations; taking account also of the individual's record of service, his general character and his academic rights. Little or no weight should be given to his personal obnoxiousness, his unpopularity or the inconvenience and annoyance caused by his conduct before investigating committees.

3. Should the individual teacher himself invoke the Fifth Amendment as ground for his refusal to testify? This is a very different question, which the individual must himself decide—on grounds of conscience and guided by legal advice. If he detests the inquisitorial methods of a committee and considers it a menace to freedom, and says in effect, "It's none of your business—I'll have nothing to do with you," he must be prepared to take the consequences. What they will be will depend on many factors, including the number of persons so resisting and the mood of public opinion. If he invokes his constitutional rights he had better be clear as to what they are before he counts on them too heavily. If he invokes the Fifth Amendment, and if he is not to expose himself to the charge of perjury, he must believe that a truthful answer to questions put to him by the committee would in fact incriminate him.

This does not imply that the teacher is using the Constitution to cover his guilt, but that he believes that his answer could be used against him, as a link in the evidence supporting a criminal charge, however innocent he may be. He may not invoke this right to avoid losing a job; nor, on the other hand, need he believe that his answers would, either in themselves or together with other evidence, establish his guilt. He need only believe that they could conceivably be considered as adverse evidence in a criminal proceeding. In the present mood of judges and juries, and under recent constitutional decisions, this is a broad ground.

He could honestly believe that in answering a question, or through one question's leading to another, he might be trapped into contradicting himself, and so create evidence on which he could be charged with perjury. But this would not justify him in the eyes of the law. He can always, when genuinely in doubt or ignorance, so testify. If the possibility of giving conflicting testimony were to be taken as a ground for refusing to testify, testimony in general would no longer be obligatory, and the innocent defendant could lose the right to subpoena witnesses in his behalf.

Finally there is no legal ground for refusing testimony on the ground that it would incriminate others. In this case there may be a conflict between the legal code and the code of personal honor, in which case the individual may be obliged to abide by honor and take the legal consequences, or abide by the law and suffer the distress of others and of his own conscience.

THE FIRST DISMISSALS [7]

Rutgers University was first in the country to fire professors for refusing to testify fully before a senatorial investigating committee.

Professors Moses I. Finley and Simon W. Heimlich, who, on different occasions refused to answer certain questions about Communist party membership posed by the Senate Internal Security Subcommittee, were released last December by action of the Board of Trustees of the state-owned school.

Defenders of the two professors charged infringement of academic freedom, but the Rutgers administration countered that refusal to talk in itself undermined this freedom.

As early as September, Rutgers had no clear policy on how to deal with this situation. Various committees were set up in turn, but when the Board of Trustees fired Finley and Heimlich, it further resolved to consider future silence of the same type "cause for immediate dismissal."

The decision was attacked by student newspapers, faculty groups, the state CIO-PAC [Political Action Committee], the American Civil Liberties Union, and others. Cries of politics, infringement of academic freedom, and hastiness were common.

President Lewis Webster Jones, however, defended the trustees' action. Those who were up in arms were confusing many issues with the one central point, he said.

The sole issue before the Faculty Committee of Review, and before the trustees, was whether, under all the circumstances, a university teacher, and a representative of this university, has an obligation to answer the questions of a legally constituted investigatory body concerning membership in the Communist party.

In March 1952, Finley, assistant professor of history at the College of Arts and Sciences, appeared before the Senate Internal

[7] From "Rutgers First to Dismiss for Fifth Amendment Use," news story. *Harvard Crimson*, Fifth Annual Academic Freedom Report. p M-2. June 10, 1953. Reprinted by permission.

Security Subcommittee. He had been accused of being a Communist by Professor Karl A. Wittfogel and William M. Canning before his appearance, and later by Bella Dodd. Their testimony, under oath, referred to a period about 1939.

Finley testified that he was not now a Communist, but refused to say whether he had ever been one. He tried to base his refusal to answer questions about past party ties on both the First and Fifth Amendments. Since the courts have held that the First Amendment cannot be used effectively without a court test of the claim, the subcommittee did not accept this ground. It did accept the Fifth Amendment.

In September 1952, Heimlich, an associate professor of physics and mathematics at the College of Pharmacy, was called before the Senate subcommittee. He refused to answer questions as to past or present Communist party membership. He also would not say whether he had ever used an alias or done recruiting for American Youth for Democracy. Heimlich based his silence on Fifth Amendment rights.

His reasons for remaining tight-lipped, he later explained, were that he believed his political, religious and other views were his private affair so long as they did not affect his conduct in the classroom, and that answers to such questions might precipitate government prosecution.

Two days after his appearance before the Jenner subcommittee, Heimlich, at the request of President Jones, issued a statement to the effect that he was not a Communist and had never been one. He also stated that he had never used an alias nor recruited for AYD. None of this information, of course, was given under oath.

Since university statutes did not cover this kind of situation, President Jones set up a special committee of faculty, trustees, and alumni to advise him of a possible course of action. After studying the cases, the committee unanimously concluded that the "refusals of Professor Heimlich to answer questions of the Senate committee relative to his connection with the Communist party, and of Professor Finley as to his previous connection with it, on the ground that to answer might tend to incriminate them, do raise a real question as to their fitness to continue as teachers on the university faculty."

This committee also urged that a special advisory committee on review, appointed by the Faculty Committee on Committees, study further and make recommendations promptly.

The Special Faculty Committee of Review rolled up its collective sleeves and went to work. Its conclusions surprised many, heartened others, angered some.

Stressing that legally the professors might use the Fifth Amendment for their protection even though they were not Communists, and that both professors were considered excellent, objective teachers, the committee unanimously advised that "no charges should be preferred against Mr. Heimlich or Mr. Finley. It therefore recommends to the President that no further action be taken."

In December, the Board of Trustees reversed the recommendation of the faculty committee and gave the two professors the choice of either going before the Senate subcommittee by the end of the month and answering its questions, or losing their jobs with Rutgers. The trustees also decided that future action of this sort be considered "cause for immediate dismissal."

Right after the trustees' decision came, an explosion followed. . . .

Many asked the trustees to reconsider their stand. The Student Council rapped the Board for having disregarded the faculty committee's proposals without refuting their arguments. . . .

In January, President Jones issued a ten-page pamphlet to quiet the clamor. The trustees, he said, did not argue with the other issues raised by the faculty committee because they considered them irrelevant. "The sole issue . . . was whether . . . a representative of [Rutgers] has an obligation to answer the questions of a legally constituted investigatory body concerning membership in the Communist party." This, and this alone, was in question.

Thus, when Finley and Heimlich refused to give a rational account of their position on communism, this "cuts the ground out from academic freedom itself."

A university, especially a state university, he said, has clear responsibilities to the community as well as to the scholarly world. . . . "Academic freedom has unfortunately become a defensive notion," Jones stated. "As such, it does not logically imply the freedom to be silent, as the Faculty Committee of Review has maintained. The freedom to be silent is a civil right guaranteed under special circumstances by the Constitution. But academic freedom entails the obligation to render an explanation, as clearly and rationally as possible, whenever such an explanation is called for by duly constituted governmental bodies acting within the limits of their authority."

A CASE HISTORY: OHIO STATE'S
PROFESSOR DARLING [8]

Early in March . . . [1953] Professor [Byron Thornwell Darling], a member of the department of physics staff since 1947, was served with a subpoena signed by the House Un-American Activities Committee, Representative Harold H. Velde, chairman. . . . He went to Washington, where . . . on Thursday, March 12, he went before the Un-American Activities Committee in a private hearing. The following morning he was called back to a public hearing and asked questions by various members of the committee.

He identified himself as working on an Air Force project . . . not regarded as secret. Then he refused to answer whether or not he had access to or was in possession of classified information. He cited the Fifth Amendment in refusing to answer. . . . He refused to say: if he is now or ever was a member of the Communist party; whether he is a member of any Communist organization at Ohio State; whether any Communists still exist on the campus; if he had ever used the assumed name of "Springer" or any other assumed name in writing or speech-making; if he had ever performed services for the Communist party for which he had not received compensation. . . .

[8] From "A Darkened Door," news story. *Ohio State University Monthly.* p5-9. April 15, 1953. Reprinted by permission.

As soon as word reached the campus that Dr. Darling had refused to answer some of the questions, President Howard L. Bevis released the following statement to the press:

Until the university can make a complete study of the record of his appearance before the Velde Committee, Professor Byron T. Darling is relieved of all duties at the Ohio State University. . . .

State Representative Samuel L. Devine, secretary of the Ohio Un-American Activities Commission, told newsmen his group "had been aware of Darling" as a subject of inquiry for more than a year; had not called him for testimony because of the "interest of other security organizations.". . .

State Auditor James A. Rhodes, entering the act, told newsmen he would not honor Darling's salary after noon on March 13 (time of the suspension) and the salary of Mrs. Darling . . . , an employee of the department of romance languages, until her status was cleared by university officials.

In the welter of such public reaction, university officials quietly went about a fair investigation of the case. A request was sent to Washington for a complete transcript of the hearing. The transcript was carefully studied. A complete check was made of the record of Professor Darling . . . at the university and at his previous posts. No communistic activity was brought to light.

When he returned to Columbus following the Washington hearing, Dr. Darling released this statement:

The Velde Un-American Activities Committee had no legitimate cause for requiring me to appear before it and for badgering me in an open session yesterday. I have never done anything disloyal and against the interest of my country. . . and the Velde Un-American Activities Committee has not produced a single shred of evidence to the contrary. I deplore the activities of this committee in its performance of a typical witch hunt against the scientists and teachers of the United States. . . .

Members of the department of physics . . . agreed unanimously. . . .

At no time during the entire period of his association with us have we had the slightest reason to doubt his loyalty to the university he serves and to his country. . . .

His students were firm in saying that never in his classroom or lab had he said or done anything that could be construed as disloyal. . . .

On March 24, President Bevis sent a letter to Professor Darling calling attention to the fact that the Ohio State loyalty oath, adopted in 1948 and which all staff members must sign, says in part: ". . . is not a member of any political party or organization that advocates the overthrow of the Government of the United States . . . nor will become a member."

. . . By this statement of policy [the President wrote] the Board of Trustees clearly implies that every employee should, as a condition of continued employment conduct himself so that he shall be able to testify on such matters without fear of self-incrimination.

Your refusal to answer the questions of the (Un-American Activities) committee raises serious doubts as to your fitness to hold the position you occupy. Doubt is raised as to your ability to answer these questions truthfully without self-incrimination. Doubt is raised as to your moral integrity. . . . There is also a serious implication of gross insubordination to university policy and of conduct clearly inimical to the best interests of the university.

He then set . . . the date for a hearing with Darling. . . . On Saturday, April 4, Professor Darling appeared before President Bevis. . . .

He stated that he is not, and never has been, a member of the Communist party or of any organization which, to his knowledge or belief, was affiliated or connected with the Communist party.

He then gave his reasons for not answering the committee's questions: (1) he felt he had the legal and moral right to refuse; (2) though innocent, he felt he was in a position of undeserved danger if he answered the questions; (3) he felt the Velde Committee's inquiry into education is a violation of the academic freedom and freedoms of speech and association guaranteed by the First Amendment. . . .

He described his dilemma:

I could not, as apparently the committee wanted me to, testify that I am or was a Communist, or disloyal, or had done anything wrong. Such testimony would have been completely false. But if I testified to the truth, then I ran the risk of being charged, and even convicted, of perjury on the basis of evidence in the committee's possession, which evidence was either false or capable of being falsely interpreted.

In ordinary times and circumstances, I probably would not have regarded this situation as presenting a serious dilemma. I would have, I think, denied the accusations, without any serious apprehension that I might, through a miscarriage of justice, be accused of committing perjury by telling the truth. But these were not ordinary times, nor was I in ordinary circumstances. . . .

Summing up, he said in part:

If you dismiss me, you do so not because I am a Communist, for I am not, but because I have relied on the Constitution. This is indeed a blow at the rights of teachers. . . .

Monday, members of the faculty received a statement of Dr. Darling's stand, in which he pointed out:

The suggested grounds of dismissal . . . are that by asserting . . . the privilege of the Fifth Amendment . . . serious doubts are raised as to my fitness to hold my position. . . .

I wish to emphasize that these charges . . . arise exclusively from my refusal to answer the questions described on the basis of the Fifth Amendment, as well as the First. No charge or suggestion is made that I have been an incompetent teacher, that I have engaged in any misconduct other than . . . my refusals to answer certain questions of the committee. No question as to my loyalty is raised except insofar as it is suggested that disloyalty may be inferred from my refusals. The same thing is true as to my integrity, morality, compliance with university requirements, and, I suppose, as to whether I am or ever have been a member of the Communist party or any other organization alleged to advocate the overthrow of the government by force and violence. . . .

He then pleaded not guilty to the charges and based his defense on two aspects:

1. that a claim of the Fifth Amendment is not, and can not be, a proper basis for finding immorality, gross insubordination, conduct clearly inimical to the best interests of the university, or, for that matter, any kind of misconduct or defect of character.

2. that not only in the abstract, but in his own particular case, the assertion of the Fifth Amendment warrants no such finding. . . .

President Bevis answered Dr. Darling's two points of defense by saying:

We are not finding fault with the Fifth Amendment. It is properly designed to give protection within specified limits. My charge is that Dr. Darling failed in his duty to the university. Against this failure the Fifth Amendment is no protection. . . .

Proceeding now to analyze the situation, the controlling issue in this whole matter is Dr. Darling's fitness to hold faculty rank in the Ohio State University. . . .

Referring to the record of his appearance before the committee it should be observed that Dr. Darling appeared not merely in his personal capacity but as an associate professor of the university. At that hearing Dr. Darling did not admit he was a Communist, but he pointedly refused to deny it, claiming the protection of the Fifth Amendment. By taking this course he involved not only his own standing and prestige, but that of the university of which he was a part.

The Fifth Amendment is indeed a guaranty that one cannot be required to make a statement which can be used as evidence against him in a criminal proceeding. But the Fifth Amendment does not refute the inferences which generally flow from public refusal to answer pertinent questions and does not prevent our consideration of the effect of such inferences in determining the fitness of Dr. Darling to hold professorial rank.

The President then referred to a recent statement approved by the American Association of Universities which said in part:

As in all acts of association the professor accepts conventions which become morally binding. Above all, he owes his colleagues in the university complete candor and integrity precluding any kind of clandestine or conspiratorial activities. He owes equal candor to the public. . . . In this respect the invocation of the Fifth Amendment places upon the professor a heavy burden of proof of his fitness to hold a teaching position and lays upon his university an obligation to re-examine his qualifications for membership in its society. . . .

Dr. Bevis pointed out:

In his personal capacity as a citizen he was free to claim the protection of the Fifth Amendment and bear whatever personal consequences might follow. But upon beginning his relationship with the university Dr. Darling assumed obligation and responsibilities to it and his colleagues. . . .

By refusing to say whether he had ever belonged to the Communist party or any related organization, whether he had ever performed services for or received funds from that party or such organizations, Dr. Darling did grave injury to the university and its faculty. By refusing to say whether certain of his colleagues were Communists he cast an unwarranted aspersion upon them individually.

These considerations lead only to the conclusion that Dr. Darling has shown his unfitness for the position he holds. They show a lack of candor and moral integrity in matters vital to his professorial status. They show gross insubordination to university policy. They show conduct clearly inimical to the best interests of the university. . . .

It is my recommendation, therefore, that Byron Thornwell Darling be discharged from his position as associate professor and from the service of the Ohio State University effective as of this date.

FINAL CHAPTER ON THE DARLING CASE [9]

The second chapter of the Darling case was written April 20, when the Board of Trustees held its regular monthly meeting on the campus. . . .

Foremost on the agenda: a recommendation by President Howard L. Bevis that Dr. Byron T. Darling be dismissed from the faculty for gross insubordination, lack of moral integrity and conduct inimical to the best interests of the university. . . .

It was a recommendation termed "shocking" by Dr. Darling, who claimed it set a precedent for assigning college professors to second-class citizenship, eligible for some rights of the Constitution, but not all.

The faculty found itself divided in its sentiment. The Conference Committee of the Teaching Staff, after a long meeting, took the view that the action was within the discretion of the President . . . but . . . asked the Board of Trustees to reject the charges of gross insubordination and immorality as basis for dismissal, unless further investigation should substantiate them, since "a great many faculty members" felt the charges not supported by evidence in the public record. . . .

The local chapter of the AAUP [American Association of University Professors], at a full-dress meeting attended by 127 (there are 992 holding professorial rank at Ohio State) . . . voted to suspend judgment on the administration disposition of the case until an investigation could be made by the national AAUP group. . . .

[9] From "The Darling Case," news story. *Ohio State University Monthly* p6-8. May 15, 1953. Reprinted by permission.

Other faculty members and off-campus observers felt that too many hairs were being split over definitions and that the faculty dissenters, in trying to make the matter an issue of academic freedom, were actually setting the cause of academic freedom back instead of helping it. . . .

Newspapers throughout the state were unanimous in their reaction. Editorial after editorial praised the university's handling of the case, had little sympathy for Dr. Darling and his behavior on the witness stand in Washington.

With these events in mind, the members of the Board of Trustees . . . weighed the evidence. . . . Their decision . . . was unanimous: approval of President Bevis' recommendation.

ACADEMIC FREEDOM VS. SURVIVAL [10]

"The plight of academic freedom" has become the genuine concern of many an intellectually honest educator in America today. There is no doubt that such a phrase as "character assassination" is taking on sinister realism. It is further obvious that a climate of suspicion and coercion is hardly conducive to right thinking and that a spirit of free inquiry needs to be maintained at the core of our institutions of learning. Upon that foundation rests our whole educational system, which in turn constitutes the cornerstone of our democracy.

This once granted, however, one is led to wonder whether the most vocal champions of academic freedom in America today are not at times overstating their case, while overlooking basic aspects of the problem. By this I mean aspects involving our very existence and survival as a free country. For surely when enemy infiltration in our national organism worms its way into atomic secrets or into our system of radar protection, radical measures have to be taken.

Human infirmity being what it is, the many ramifications or implications of such measures are bound to hurt here and there, or at least inconvenience innocent bystanders. At such times, however, a mere consideration of the issue at hand should make

[10] From "To Protect Education," letter to the editor, by Emile Caillet, Stuart professor of Christian philosophy, Princeton Theological Seminary. New York Times. p E8. October 18, 1953. Reprinted by permission.

one sober. To be specific, the uneasiness of a college professor unfairly suspected is to be deplored. Yet the fall of an H-bomb in New York or Los Angeles is a likelihood belonging to quite another order of magnitude.

It is a sad fact—one, by the way, which academic men may observe in their own institutions—that the most liberal regime will always suffer because of delinquency on the part of a few, or even of a single individual in the community. It takes but two or three cheaters to ruin an honor system.

Taking the deeper view, then, it will readily appear that the crisis of academic freedom must be ascribed to the moral and spiritual delinquency of a few. This being the case, the solution is to try and dispose of the evil-doers within the context of the best available code of professional ethics. Health of any organism will always imply an adequate treatment of the cause of disease. So much more in our present situation, when survival is at stake.

While deploring the fact that investigation has too often become synonymous with guilt, I fail to see why anyone with a clear conscience should refuse to answer questions, but rather seek to hide behind technicalities and intricacies. One of the unexpected blessings of our last national election and related constitution of a new cabinet has been the admission that public men should be willing at all times to lay bare their record and henceforth live in a glass house, as it were, while they continue in public office. None of those concerned to my knowledge has ever complained of an inherent infringement upon his freedom.

American educators stand at the forefront of public life. Theirs has become a crucial responsibility at a time like this. Let them, therefore, fully and candidly cooperate with those immediately responsible for our welfare and survival. This will be the best way of protecting and promoting academic freedom. It is high time, moreover, to expose the fallacy that a man has got to be "pink" in order to deserve the name of a true liberal.

An overwhelming majority of academic men feel the way I do in this, I am sure. Yet their massive testimony is not heard, simply because they have no complaint. They rest satisfied to enjoy the blessings of this haven of freedom we call America. I would beg leave to suggest that they also should become vocal, so that the public at large may gain a truer perspective on the academic world.

THE BROADER ISSUE—ACADEMIC FREEDOM

EDITOR'S INTRODUCTION

Throughout all of the discussion thus far, the subject of academic freedom crops up repeatedly. It forms the basis of most of the protest against congressional investigations, against loyalty oaths, against administrative dismissal policies centering on the use of the Fifth Amendment by witnesses. The meaning of the term "academic freedom," therefore, becomes all-important.

Leo Rockwell of Colgate University describes academic freedom in an article in the *American Association of University Professors Bulletin* as a term borrowed more than a hundred years ago from the old German universities which attracted so many young American scholars of the early nineteenth century. The German concept of a university was the search for knowledge, predicated upon two necessary conditions: freedom of learning for the student, and freedom of teaching for the teacher.

Neither of these freedoms, according to Rockwell, were known to the American colleges in the early part of the nineteenth century. Faculties and school administrators were hired or fired without question, and the notion that students should enjoy any special freedom to learn in a manner they might determine would have been considered ridiculous. Likewise, freedom to teach was almost nonexistent. Rockwell points out that by 1885, academic freedom included only the first half of the old German concept: freedom to learn, although it still didn't exist to any realistic degree. By 1899, however, academic freedom had come to include freedom to teach as well. But it wasn't until the outbreak of World War I, when faculties split on pro-Allied and pro-German lines, with many pro-Germans being fired arbitrarily, that academic freedom (as freedom to teach) received any real impetus. The American Association of University Professors was formed in 1915, and quickly took up cudgels in defense of "academic freedom."

Over a period of years the American Association of University Professors has waged a continuing campaign to secure acceptance of the principle of academic freedom by boards of regents, school administrators and the public. To a large extent it has been successful. Part of its fight has included the question of permanent tenure, the right of a faculty member after a certain period of time to job security, so that he may be discharged only upon proof of violation of university codes and only upon action of his colleagues.

Firing of college professors without cause, or because of unpopular opinions, has been a focus of attention for the AAUP fight for academic freedom. Instances such as that in Kansas this year, where a college president fired an instructor for signing a petition seeking an amnesty for the eleven Communist leaders convicted under the Smith Act, have been bitterly opposed by the professors' national organization. And the policy expressed by the acting president of Emporia State Teachers College, where the firing occurred, has long been a matter of contention: "it has been long accepted in the teacher's code of ethics that any teacher who wishes to enter the political arena would sever his connection with his institution either by resignation or by leave of absence." Most major universities today concede the right of a faculty member to participate in political affairs without penalty, but many smaller schools still cling to the older point of view. Such attitudes have little to do with the current Communist issue, except that charges of communism often unsupported by proof have been sufficient to lead to dismissal in various institutions throughout the nation. And the AAUP, in attacking any arbitrary firing of a college professor, for whatever reason, is merely trying to establish more firmly the principle that no member of a college faculty should be removed without a hearing, that he should be judged by his colleagues, and that mere evidence of political activity should not be sufficient grounds for dismissal. This, then, is the background for the concern over academic freedom which arises from the current congressional investigations and the loyalty oath cases.

ACADEMIC FREEDOM DEFINED [1]

There has never been so much commotion over the freedom of the scholar or the educator as there is in this country today. In the past there has indeed been less, much less, academic freedom—for in the ages of authority it was at best a very limited affair. But never in modern times has there been so massive and many-sided an assault upon it. Many of these assaults have been repelled, but more than a few have succeeded. All across the country there are groups that, under one banner or another, are seeking to limit it. Dozens of organizations are "investigating" it, including at present three congressional bodies. There is not a single important institution of learning that has not been the object of some accusation concerning it. There is scarcely a college or university president who has not run into some troubles over it.

What *is* this academic freedom? What is its importance? Why is there so much concern over it? These things need to be explained, for the people are being misled about these questions, and even some educators are by no means sufficiently alert to the situation.

Academic freedom means the freedom of the educator to do his proper work, to fulfill his function, to render to his society the special service that he has to offer. His work is to learn and to teach, and this is what every genuine scholar wants above all to do. That is what he is appointed to do. That is what the institution of learning is for. Here lies its unique function, its primary mission in society.

Every major type of social organization has its own unique function which requires an appropriate range of freedom to fulfill. The church aspires to one. The family another. So also the academy, the college or the university. Academic freedom then is the freedom of the men of the academy, the faculty members, within their various areas of competence, in the field of learning and teaching.

Observe that this freedom is not the freedom to express opinions on any matter under the sun. In a democratic country

[1] From "The Freedom to Search for Knowledge," by Robert M. MacIver, sociologist, Columbia University Academic Freedom Project Director. New York *Times Magazine*. April 12, 1953. p 12+. Reprinted by permission.

that is the freedom of the citizen. What we're talking about is a special form of freedom derived from a special function—the freedom proper to the member of a particular profession, without which the calling is perverted and falsified and the service it renders is betrayed. Just as the medical man needs a particular area of freedom for his work, or the man of law, so does the man of the academy.

The effort to seek and impart knowledge means a limit to the control of any external authority over the institution of learning. Where this freedom exists, no authority can say: "This is the truth, this is what you must teach." Or: "This is the truth; if your investigations lead you to doubt it or to deny it, you must refrain from doing so."

It is the freedom to reach conclusions through scholarly investigation. It does not imply the freedom to *act* according to your conclusions, if such action is against the law. It is emphatically not a freedom to conspire to overthrow government or to incite others to do so. But it embraces the freedom of the serious student of government to reach and express conclusions regarding its nature and regarding the good or evil results of this or that form of government.

Academic freedom is at the same time a high responsibility. It is not a privilege possessed by an academic guild. It is not a concession granted by a government or by a community to an enclave of scholars. It is claimed as a necessity, not a luxury; as a condition of service, not as a social award. As we shall presently see, it is a fundamental condition of a free society.

Some enemies of this freedom say: "We are perfectly willing to let the teacher do his job. His job is to impart information— we don't in the least want to interfere with that. What we object to is when the teacher throws his weight around and starts indoctrinating his students. That's not his business. By all means let him give the students any knowledge he has, but let him keep to the facts and keep his valuations out of it. We don't pay him to teach values, especially values contrary to our own."

This sounds plausible—perhaps even reasonable. But let's see how it works out. Suppose for example, you are a teacher of English literature. What would confining yourself to "the facts" mean? What sort of understanding would you convey of a play of Shakespeare or say, Walt Whitman's poems if you confined yourself to "the facts"? Would it not deaden any incipient interest the student might have, or at the least deaden his interest in you, unless you did a bit of interpretation? And if you do that, you are no longer giving "the facts."

Or suppose you are an economist and you're talking about inflation. Would you reel off changing index numbers and stop there, or would you analyze inflation as a problem? If the latter, are you confining yourself to "the facts"? Are you even steering clear of "values"?

Or you are a sociologist and you're discussing, say, a housing shortage in some part of the country. But why call it a shortage? A shortage is not a "fact" but a conclusion you believe to be borne out by the evidence. And why deal with it at all if you're eschewing values altogether? The facts are of interest because they have meaning for us. If you exclude the meaning your teaching is dead. If you include it you cannot altogether exclude values.

He who seeks knowledge is seeking the connections between things. He is not interested in mere detached items of information. He wants to find out how things are related. His mere opinions do not count and he should not foist them on his students. But he should be free to express any conclusions he reaches as a result of his study in his own field, explaining how he reaches them. His conclusions may be faulty, but there is no other road to knowledge. Nor is there any other way to education since the teacher is out to train the student's mind, not to load his memory with undigestible "facts."

This, then, is the freedom the scholar needs, the freedom that is now on the defensive. Why is it important? Why does it matter much to anyone but the scholar? Why should the people, too, be concerned if this freedom is threatened or abridged?

Academic freedom is important to us all because knowledge is important, because the search for knowledge is important, and because the spirit in the search for knowledge is most important of all. . . .

The search for knowledge has again a value outside of the direct rewards it brings. Anything we know, we know only in part, and many things we think we know are not knowledge.

At one time men knew the earth was flat and that the heavenly bodies revolved around the earth. Until recently Newtonian physics, itself a tremendous advance, was the last word in knowledge. But there is never a last word. To the seeker after truth all horizons are eternally open. He is the enemy of all the hard, proud dogmatisms that fasten on the minds of men and breed intolerance and sharp division between group and group, between people and people, between nation and nation.

The business of the university is not so much the guardianship of knowledge as the search for knowledge, the keeping open of the intellectual horizon. This service is invaluable. The one institution supremely dedicated to the spread of enlightenment is the institution of learning. Its individual members have interests and prejudices and passions like other men. They go wrong like other men. But together, each in his own field, they seek for knowledge, and thus the institution is redeemed. It is the belief in the supreme importance of the freedom to seek knowledge which unites them.

Without that belief and its triumphant vindication in our colleges and universities the right of a man to think for himself, to inquire, to have his own opinions, would lack any sure foundation. Democracy, in a world of incessantly whirling propaganda, would have no strong defense. And civilization, what remained of it, would become no more than a mesh of techniques designed for the enslavement of body and mind, as it was in Hitler's Germany, as it is in Soviet Russia.

Only the spirit that animates the endless search for knowledge can save us from these things. This spirit must continue to flourish outside our universities as well as within their walls. It is the same spirit that keeps the press free. It is back of the democratic willingness to let the views of every group be decently heard. It is the spirit that repudiates the right of the state or the church or any other bodies to establish a censorship over the expression of opinion or the freedom of inquiry.

It is now endangered. In every society there are always those who, fearful for their interests or secure in their dogmatisms, are ready to suppress or to control the search for knowledge. In ours today they have found a formidable new weapon.

Under the guise of protecting us from communism they employ a Communist technique to further their own interest to acquire capital or economic advantage. They brand as "red" or "pink" or "subversive" or at the least "un-American" everything they happen to dislike, whether it be progressive education or state hospitals or anti-discrimination laws or social insurance or a policy toward China different from their own or Keynesian economics or the United Nations.

The real danger besetting academic freedom—and indeed the fundamental freedom of thought, opinion, and inquiry in every form—comes from the misdirection of legitimate fears of communism and the deliberate exploitation of those fears. Communism has at this stage no influence whatever in our institutions of learning, and even in the heyday of the thirties its influence was insignificant in the great majority of these institutions.

The danger in this direction is grossly exaggerated—for whatever purposes. Attacks on academic freedom have increased on the specious ground that faculties need protection from Communist infiltration. Our colleges are perfectly capable of protecting themselves.

THE THREAT TO ACADEMIC FREEDOM [2]

Just how much interference with academic freedom has there been? Is it true, as some liberals believe, that the nation is in the "grip of a deadly reign of terror or hysteria" which threatens the maintenance of academic freedom, indeed of freedom itself?

A group of newspaper editors, in reply to a recent inquiry from the American Civil Liberties Union, concluded that academic freedom was holding its own in most places. The 1952 report of Committee A of the American Association of University Professors, made last spring, indicated that in adherence to

[2] From "An Intellectual Iron Curtain," by Francis H. Horn, executive secretary, Association for Higher Education, National Education Association. *National Education Association Journal.* 42:152-5. March 1953. Reprinted by permission.

academic freedom and tenure, "more institutions have thus far resisted than have yielded to unwholesome public pressure." It reported no significant increase in dismissals of professors or administrators involving academic freedom.

Such dismissals, however, are not the major measure of the threat to academic freedom. The great danger lies in the curtailment of freedom of thought and expression on the part of college faculties. In 1951, a New York *Times* survey revealed "a subtle, creeping paralysis of thought and speech . . . limiting both students and faculty in the area traditionally reserved for the free exploration of knowledge and truth."

Two years ago Robert M. Hutchins declared that "everywhere in the United States, university professors, whether or not they have tenure, are silenced by the general atmosphere of repression that now prevails." He spoke of the "creeping miasma of intimidation" as the most lamentable aspect of the current situation.

Is this an exaggeration? Are professors afraid to speak their minds? To support worthy but unpopular causes? To follow truth wherever it may lead? Evidence is increasing that they are. The situation is growing worse, not better.

President Harold Taylor of Sarah Lawrence College in January 1953 indicated that in recent visits to a number of college campuses, he had found "quite a few" well-respected faculty members who were unwilling to speak at public meetings on controversial issues. Carroll Newsom, associate commissioner of education for New York State, in speaking on the same program with President Taylor, declared that under the prevailing philosophies of fear professors are ignoring all controversial issues—not only those connected with communism, but those concerned with social or economic subjects that might be unpopular. Afraid to be labeled as "red" or "pink," they tend to stay in the middle of the road, playing it safe.

Norman Cousins recently reported a conversation with some faculty members who admitted reluctantly that more and more professors are afraid to "stick their necks out" and give the facts as they understand them. Rather the tendency is to "try to figure out what the big investigations will be about two years from now and then teach things today that will look good later. . . . More and more of us are doing exactly what they are doing in Russia. We're finding out what's politically safe and sticking to it."

This is the real threat to academic freedom. If this trend toward "safe" thinking and teaching, toward intellectual conformity with what certain elements of our people consider acceptable, continues, the greatness of America's colleges and universities is doomed. The institutions will continue to function, but they will no longer be contributing significantly through the advancement of knowledge and the transmission of our heritage of freedom to the general welfare of this nation and the world.

THE UNIVERSITIES' STAND ON ACADEMIC FREEDOM [3]

For three hundred years higher education has played a leading role in the advancement of American civilization. No country in history so early perceived the importance of that role and none has derived such widespread benefits from it. . . .

The modern university . . . is a unique type of organization. For many reasons it must differ from a corporation created for the . . . purpose of producing a salable article for profit. Its internal structure, procedures and discipline are properly quite different from those of business organizations. It is not so closely integrated and there is no such hierarchy of authority as is appropriate to a business concern; the permanent members of a university are essentially . . . equals.

Like its medieval prototype the modern American university is an association of individual scholars. Their effectiveness, both as scholars and as teachers, requires the capitalizing of their individual passion for knowledge and their individual competence to pursue it and communicate it to others. They are united in

[3] From "The Rights and Responsibilities of Universities and Their Faculties," policy statement issued by the Association of American Universities, March 30, 1953. (Reprinted in *United States News & World Report.* 34:65-7. April 10, 1953; also New York *Times.* p 12. March 31, 1953. Passages of the statement dealing with other aspects of academic freedom are reprinted on p 128-30 of this book.)

loyalty to the ideal of learning, to the moral code, to the country and its form of government. They represent diversified fields of knowledge; they express many points of view. Even within the same department of instruction there are not only specialists in various phases of the subject but men with widely differing interests and outlook.

Free enterprise is as essential to intellectual as to economic progress.

A university must, therefore, be hospitable to an infinite variety of skills and viewpoints, relying upon open competition among them, as the surest safeguard of truth. Its whole spirit requires investigation, criticism and presentation of ideas in an atmosphere of freedom and mutual confidence. This is the real meaning of "academic" freedom. It is essential to the achievement of its ends that the faculty of a university be guaranteed this freedom by its governing board, and that the reasons for the guarantee be understood by the public. To enjoin uniformity of outlook upon a university faculty would put a stop to learning at the source. To censor individual faculty members would put a stop to learning at its outlet.

For these reasons a university does not take an official position of its own either on disputed questions of scholarship or on political questions or matters of public policy. It refrains from so doing not only in its own but in the public interest, to capitalize the search for knowledge for the benefit of society, to give the individuals pursuing that search the freest possible scope and the greatest possible encouragement in their efforts to preserve the learning of the past and advance learning in the present. . . .

To fulfill their function, the members of university faculties must continue to analyze, test, criticize and reassess existing institutions and beliefs, approving when the evidence supports them and disapproving when the weight of evidence is on the other side. Such investigations cannot be confined to the physical world; the acknowledged fact that moral, social and political progress have not kept pace with mastery of the physical world shows the need for more intensified research, fresh insights, vigorous criticism and inventiveness. The scholar's mission requires the study and examination of unpopular ideas, of ideas considered abhorrent and even dangerous. For, just as in the case of deadly disease or the military potential of an enemy, it is only by intense study and research that the nature and extent of the danger can be understood and defenses against it perfected.

Timidity must not lead the scholar to stand silent when he ought to speak, particularly in the field of his competence. In matters of conscience and when he has truth to proclaim the scholar has no obligation to be silent in the face of popular disapproval. Some of the great passages in the history of truth have involved the open challenge of popular prejudice in times of tension such as those in which we live.

What applies to research applies equally to teaching. So long as an instructor's observations are scholarly and germane to his subject, his freedom of expression in his classroom should not be curbed. The university student should be exposed to competing opinions and beliefs in every field, so that he may learn to weigh them and gain maturity of judgment. Honest and skillful exposition of such opinions and beliefs is the duty of every instructor; and it is equally his privilege to express his own critical opinion and the reasons for holding it. In teaching, as in research, he is limited by the requirements of citizenship, of professional competence and good taste. Having met those standards, he is entitled to all the protection the full resources of the university can provide. . . .

Appointment to a university position and retention after appointment require not only professional competence but involve the affirmative obligation of being diligent and loyal in citizenship. Above all, a scholar must have integrity and independence. This renders impossible adherence to such a regime as that of Russia and its satellites. No person who accepts or advocates such principles and methods has any place in a university. Since present membership in the Communist party requires the acceptance of these principles and methods, such membership extinguishes the right to a university position. Moreover, if an instructor follows communistic practice by becoming a propagandist for one opinion, adopting a "party line," silencing criticism or impairing freedom of thought and expression in his classroom, he forfeits not only all university support but his right to membership in the university.

"Academic freedom" is not a shield for those who break the law. Universities must cooperate fully with law-enforcement officers whose duty requires them to prosecute those charged with offenses. Under a well-established American principle, their innocence is to be assumed until they have been convicted, under due process, in a court of proper jurisdiction.

Unless a faculty member violates a law, however, his discipline or discharge is a university responsibility and should not be assumed by political authority. Discipline on the basis of irresponsible accusations or suspicion can never be condoned. It is as damaging to the public welfare as it is to academic integrity. The university is competent to establish a tribunal to determine the facts and fairly judge the nature and degree of any trespass upon academic integrity, as well as to determine the penalty such trespass merits.

As the professor is entitled to no special privileges in law, so also he should be subject to no special discrimination. Universities are bound to deprecate special loyalty tests which are applied to their faculties but to which others are not subjected. Such discrimination does harm to the individual and even greater harm to his university and the whole cause of education by destroying faith in the ideals of university scholarship.

Finally, we assert that freedom of thought and speech is vital to the maintenance of the American system and is essential to the general welfare. Condemnation of communism and its protagonists is not to be interpreted as readiness to curb social, political, or economic investigation and research. To insist upon complete conformity to current beliefs and practices would do infinite harm to the principle of freedom, which is the greatest, the central, American doctrine. Fidelity to that principle has made it possible for the universities of America to confer great benefits upon our society and our country. Adherence to that principle is the only guarantee that the nation may continue to enjoy those benefits.

AAUP STATEMENT OF PRINCIPLES [4]

Institutions of higher education are conducted for the common good and not to further the interest of either the individual teacher or the institution as a whole. The common good depends upon the free search for truth and its free exposition.

Academic freedom is essential to these purposes and applies to both teaching and research. Academic freedom in its teaching aspect is fundamental for the protection of the rights of the teacher in teaching and of the student to freedom in learning. It carries with it duties correlative with rights.

Tenure is a means to certain ends: specifically: (1) Freedom of teaching and research and of extramural activities, and (2) A sufficient degree of economic security to make the profession attractive to men and women of ability. Freedom and economic security, hence tenure, are indispensable to the success of an institution in fulfilling its obligations to its students and to society. . . .

The teacher is entitled to freedom in the classroom in discussing his subject, but he should be careful not to introduce into his teaching controversial matter which has no relation to his subject. . . . The college or university teacher is a citizen, a member of a learned profession, and an officer of an educational institution. When he speaks or writes as a citizen, he should be free from institutional censorship or discipline, but his special position in the community imposes special obligations. As a man of learning and an educational officer, he should remember that the public may judge his profession and his institution by his utterances. Hence he should at all times be accurate, should exercise appropriate restraint, should show respect for the opinions of others, and should make every effort to indicate that he is not an institutional spokesman.

After the expiration of a probationary period teachers or investigators should have permanent or continuous tenure, and their services should be terminated only for adequate cause. . . .

[4] From "1940 Statement of Principles" on academic freedom and tenure of the American Association of University Professors. *American Association of University Professors Bulletin*. 39:122-2. Spring 1953. Reprinted by permission. (Passages of the 1953 AAUP resolution are reprinted on p 64-5, 119-20, and 138-9 of this book.)

In all cases where the facts are in dispute, the accused teacher should be informed before the hearing in writing of the charges against him and should have the opportunity to be heard in his own defense by all bodies that pass judgment upon his case.

THE UNIVERSITY'S RESPONSIBILITY TO ITS FACULTY [5]

As the principles and practices of the free mind have been slowly worked out in our democratic society, it has often happened that individuals and institutions devoted to the pursuit of truth have refused to submit to the imposition of ecclesiastical or political controls over personal beliefs or the communication of those beliefs. The issue raised by that refusal has taken one of its most controversial forms when the authorities of church or state have required, with varying kinds of inquisition, that an individual should make compulsory disclosure of his opinions or of his association with others in the advocacy of those opinions. Over and over again, in the history of our Western society, individuals and groups have challenged that requirement, have decided, even under the threat of severe penalties, that they could not loyally submit to it.

In the course of the long struggle against suppression, individual freedom has won great victories. Both the churches and the universities have fought for and have secured decisive limitations of the jurisdiction of legislative and other government agencies. The greatest of all among those victories is recorded in the First Amendment to our Constitution by which our own government forbids its Congress to take any action which would abridge the freedom of religion, speech, press, assembly, or petition. The basic meaning of that enactment is that all citizens, scholars or nonscholars, as they deal with the issues of religion or of politics, shall be unhindered by the intimidation or control of any governing agency. They must be free to follow the truth wherever it may seem to them to lead.

[5] From "Integrity of the Universities—How to Defend It," by Alexander Meiklejohn, professor emeritus of the University of Wisconsin and noted philosopher and educator. *Bulletin of the Atomic Scientists.* 9:193-4. June 1953. Reprinted by permission.

The most striking contribution of the universities to the winning of the freedom of the mind is, however, that they have gone far beyond mere resistance to the external authority of the civil government. They have, also, following the lead of the Federal Government, limited the use of their own authority. They have seen that, in universities as they are now organized, administrative actions upon appointments, salaries, promotions, dismissals, and so on, might be used, consciously or unconsciously, to influence and control the opinions and expressions of scholars and teachers. And since nothing worse than this could happen to a university, they have taken careful precautions against such abuse of their own powers. Those precautionary self-limitations are what we call, "The System of Academic Tenure." Their purpose is not to grant special favors to faculty members. It is to guard the independence and integrity of the university's own work.

The tenure system, as usually adopted, makes two sets of provisions. First, it arranges that no one shall be given "permanent tenure" on the teaching staff until his moral and intellectual competence has been tested and approved by his colleagues, on the basis of years of active service. But, second, when permanent status is thus granted to a professor, it is also provided that no adverse action shall be taken against him, except on charges of moral and intellectual incompetence, carefully defined in advance and carefully investigated by competent colleagues. These provisions give assurance that neither the threat of dismissal nor of any other administrative action will ever be used to terrify faculty members, to impose upon them an intellectual or religious or political orthodoxy. An institution which would require such orthodoxy could not be a university—that is what the tenure system means.

Committees of the Federal legislature are now attempting to impose upon faculty members the demand that they make compulsory disclosure of their beliefs and associations. And some of the scholars and teachers who have been questioned under this procedure have refused to "cooperate," have denied the authority of the committees to demand an answer to their questions. These "protestants" have, therefore, been held to be in "contempt" of Congress and have been recommended for prosecution and, if convicted, for punishment. Where that situation has arisen, what is the duty of a university toward a "protesting" professor to whom it has granted permanent tenure? . . .

It must, of course, be recognized that the refusal to "co-operate" with a governing agency will incur popular disapproval. The beliefs under investigation are, generally, regarded as dangerous and evil. A protestant's refusal to share in what seems to him a futile or unconstitutional method of rooting them out arouses, therefore, a double hostility. It outrages prevailing anxieties. It appears to defy established authority.

For the reason just stated, it is sometimes suggested that a teacher who holds fast to his conviction that legislative committees are exceeding their authority, is, thereby, doing harm to his university by arousing resentment against it. But in reply to that it must be said that no university can play its proper part in the life of a community unless it can be trusted to meet such resentment . . . without yielding because of terror. And, further, it must be said that the only serious injury which any teacher can do to his university is that he submit his mind or his words to external domination, whether by the government or any other institution. . . .

But the decisive element in the situation is the clear fact that a citizen-scholar of the United States may honestly, intelligently, loyally, believe that the intent of the Constitution forbids him to submit to the requirement of compulsory disclosure of his beliefs. The question of the constitutional relation between a citizen and his legislature is as difficult as it is important. . . .

From what has just been said it follows that no university is called upon to decide whether a protesting professor is right or wrong in his refusal to "cooperate." Any genuine institution of learning accepts diversity of opinion on such controversial issues as a fruitful feature of its work. And this means that, for an institution which has adopted a tenure system, the only relevant question is "Has this man, by his protest, given evidence of any of these forms of moral or intellectual incompetence which are agreed upon as the only justifications of disciplinary action against him?" If such evidence is lacking, a genuine university will stand by its accredited representative, as it is pledged to do. And if any other agency, governmental or non-governmental, attempts to discipline him, such a university will not supinely acquiesce, will not consent to or share in the violation of those principles upon which its very existence, as a servant of the truth, depends.

ACADEMIC RESPONSIBILITIES [6]

If at times it appears that our university colleagues protest overly much about "academic freedom," they do so because it is the one indispensable condition of their existence. Without it, their professional careers, the purposes to which they have dedicated their lives, would become meaningless. Either we have academic freedom or academic slavery. There is no middle ground for a true university.

But academic freedom, like all other freedoms, ultimately will be lost to its possessors unless they deserve to keep it. And freedom is undeserved and forever insecure unless it is set within a solid framework of responsibility. It is more pleasant, always, to talk of freedom and rights than of duties and obligations. Unhappily, some of our academic brethren who are first to man the ramparts in defense of freedom seem less eager to talk of those responsibilities which are the precondition for the freedom which they defend.

Academic responsibility means for the individual that he accepts fully, and without reservation, his obligations to the community of scholars of which he is a part. His first obligation is that of complete honesty in his work. While no man is entirely free from bias and prejudice, the scholar's goal must be that of impartiality and objectivity, both in his research and his teaching. He must be prepared to accept any conclusions which are dictated by his work and his own rational judgment thereon. If he has

[6] From the address by Dr. Grayson Kirk, president of Columbia University, delivered at the 199th Columbia Commencement, June 3, 1953. New York *Times*. p34. June 3, 1953. Reprinted by permission.

committed himself to membership in any totalitarian group which dictates beforehand the conclusions which he may draw from his work, he has no right to ask a society of scholars to keep him in their midst, to protect him. He has disowned the basic principle on which his society operates. . . .

A second responsibility of the scholar is that of honesty to his colleagues. He has no right to expect them to protect him, as a member of their community, unless his relations with them are those of complete candor both as to his organizational affiliations and his fundamental beliefs. Intellectual deceit, falsehood, or even evasion, are no proper baggage for a scholar. This does not mean that a scholar must be prepared to bare his soul in any requested way to his colleagues; it does mean that if he has assumed intellectual obligations which are inconsistent with the honest exercise of his profession, he owes it to his colleagues to disclose this fact; otherwise he is an imposter and a fraud.

Finally a scholar cannot evade the general responsibilities which derive from his institutional associations. He must be asked to suppress an honest view of any subject, but he must always be asked to remember that his membership in the community makes it impossible for him to speak entirely as a private citizen with no imputation of institutional association. He cannot, in good conscience, ask the general public to listen to him on certain occasions as Professor John Doe of Columbia University and on others merely as citizen John Doe. Whatever he does, whatever he says, and on any or all occasions, will to some degree involve the academic society of which he is a part. He must comport himself under all circumstances so as to reflect credit upon the judgment of the community which asked him to become a member of it. This may at times be an irksome obligation but a man who is unwilling to assume it has no right to clamor about academic freedom.

For the university community as a whole, academic responsibility means, first of all, that all three segments of the permanent group—the trustees, faculty and administration—will jointly share the obligations to uphold the standards of the community and to eliminate those individuals who have failed to meet the tests of membership. I do not believe that general rules should be applied to such cases, nor do I believe in any automatic or hasty action, but I do believe profoundly that the scholarly community must be prepared through proper procedures to eliminate its unfit if it asks society to respect academic freedom. We must not allow our traditional professional tolerance for diverse opinions to cause us to be duped by those who have sworn allegiance to beliefs which are the antithesis of all that we stand for. Academic freedom is only for free men.

THE CLOSED-MIND DOCTRINE [7]

Academic freedom, it is agreed, is a precious possession. It is so precious that the congressional committee wishes to protect it; so precious that the American Association of University Professors wishes to protect it; so precious that even presidents and boards of trustees deny they are violating it—and yet professors get fired or are suspended, even though they follow sound legal advice when they appear before the committee.

What is really alleged by administrators is not that the offending instructor is romantically a conspirator against the peace and dignity of the United States; what is usually now said is that, by virtue of being a member of the Communist party, the offending instructor has a closed mind and is therefore no longer fit to teach.

This is very attractive doctrine. It carries considerable weight and immensely simplifies the administrative problem. It gives the administrator a great moral advantage, and takes every advantage, both moral and intellectual, away from the man who is fired. He has no possible retort. If you are classified as belonging to a category of citizens whose minds are closed, it is clear that you do not belong in the academic community, where minds are supposed to be open. But I strongly infer from my own experience and observation, after a lifetime of teaching, that the

    [7] From "How Much Academic Freedom?" by Howard Mumford Jones, professor of English at Harvard and president of the American Academy of Arts and Sciences from 1944 to 1951. *Atlantic Monthly.* 191:36-40. June 1953. Reprinted by permission.

first criterion of an open mind is not to make absolute statements about men.

The one sure fact in the general uproar is that very few persons are going to admit to being Communists. What, then, is the administrator to do, if he is to avoid closed minds? There is, of course, the loyalty oath; but if anything is clear from experience with loyalty oaths, it is that they do not automatically produce loyalty. Or is the administrator to refer every teaching appointment to the FBI? I imagine the FBI would be the first to complain. Or shall he hire some private detective agency paid out of college funds donated by the alumni?

Moreover, it is not merely the known Communist (if you can discover him) who is to be denied appointment because he has a closed mind; it is the potential Communist who is not going to be hired—that is, anybody upon whom somebody else can, as we say, hang something. Even the conservative New York *Times*, in the articles on education which appear in its Sunday issues, recently noted how the intellectual life of our campuses has declined in vigor with the growth of investigations into education, government, science, and what not. Students, especially as they near the time they must go into the army or into employment, find it is a whole lot wiser not to express dangerous thoughts. Fear of being suspected of leanings towards the left has closed the mind and shut the lips of youth in our time. As a young friend of mine was told the other day by an older student: "Don't join anything—then they can't get you into trouble ten years from now."

The simple principle that you can, a priori and arbitrarily, distinguish a whole class of persons whose minds are permanently closed on all subjects, and set them apart from other persons, whose minds are not closed, seems to me so mischievous a principle, so laden with eventual disaster, that I vigorously dissent from it. Here, as in other areas, circumstances alter cases; here, as in any other crucial problem of academic life, the individual case must be studied; here, as in all matters of appointment and promotion, we must take into account the totality of components in the personal problem—professional training, teaching skill, personality, promise. It is this coming back to the individual and studying him in his professional context that has made the American college or university a great institution as compared with what it was when, for example, economic or theological orthodoxy was made the primary test for teaching in the universities.

How quickly we forget! As late as 1897 President Andrews of Brown was forced to resign because he had a closed mind on the gold standard. It is true, he was later reinstated, whereas Dr. Weinberg of the University of Minnesota, acquitted of perjury by a trial jury in March, has been informed that he will not be reinstated because he refused to cooperate with Federal authorities! What good is acquittal in such cases if the academic world refuses to recognize the implication of law?

What *is* academic freedom? Whatever it is, we shall not nourish it, we shall not protect it, by laying down the rule that such and such persons are unemployable by reason of their past associations or their present interests. We shall neither nourish it nor protect it by exalting the morality of the state above the morality of the individual conscience. We shall not nourish it, we shall not protect it, by assuming that all members of a party we hate are wicked and evil persons. We shall not nourish it, we shall not protect it, by abandoning, even in this day of the cold war, the traditional wise doctrine of toleration for persons whose views we detest and whose practices are almost invariably wrong. Annoying as Communists are, baffling to the democratic process as their tactics have proved, right though it be to trace out and bring to publicity their devious ways, I for one rest defiantly upon the great paragraph of Mr. Justice Holmes in his dissenting opinion of 1918, when five Russian-born Communists were sentenced to imprisonment for distributing leaflets in New York City— leaflets which a majority of the Supreme Court found to be incentives to bring about a change of government by force and violence. Justices Brandeis and Holmes could not agree that there was any clear and present danger in this act, and Mr. Justice Holmes wrote these memorable words:

When men have realized that time has upset many fighting faiths, they may come to believe even more than they believe the very foundations of their own conduct that the ultimate good desired is better reached by free trade in ideas—that the best test of truth is the power of the thought to get itself accepted in the competition of the market, and that truth is the only ground upon which their wishes safely can be carried out. . . . I think that we should be eternally vigilant against attempts to check the expression of opinions that we loathe and believe to be fraught with death, unless they so imminently threaten immediate interference with the lawful and pressing purposes of the law that an immediate check is required to save the country.

I am not persuaded by anything I have read or know that the presence of a few Communists among the teaching profession in this country constitutes an emergency; I cannot agree that the refusal to incriminate one's self before an investigating committee is *per se* proper ground for wrecking the professional life of a teacher, however foolish I may think he is. . . . Unless some unforeseen turn of events should alter the present posture of affairs, I believe that long-run wisdom in the United States is to leave reason free to combat error.

A BUSINESSMAN'S VIEW OF ACADEMIC FREEDOM [8]

"Academic freedom" and the "loyalty oath" were two phrases I had seen often, but frankly they seemed unimportant in a world threatened by communism and communistic aggression. . . . If anything, the refusal of college faculties to sign a "loyalty oath" because it threatened "academic freedom" seemed a lame excuse. I assumed that I would not hesitate to sign a loyalty oath. . . . Why should a professor refuse to sign?

That was my attitude up to a few weeks ago, yet today I would openly defend the professor who refused to sign a loyalty oath and I would support him in his pleas for "academic freedom."

Why the conversion? . . . Political chicanery and propaganda had successfully changed "academic freedom" to mean a cloak to protect communism, Communists, and left-wing sympathizers on

[8] From *Academic Freedom Opened My Eyes,* pamphlet by William Kostka, president of the public relations firm of William Kostka and Associates, former managing editor of *Look.* 9p. 1953. (Also in the Roundup Section, Denver *Post.* July 12, 1953.) Reprinted by permission.

college campuses and, like many other Americans, I had accepted that meaning.

The full impact of that twisted definition and what it had done to college faculties came to me during a public relations conference at my own alma mater, Knox College in Galesburg, Illinois, a liberal arts college that for 116 years has been noted for its educational distinction and integrity. . . . Included in the agenda . . . [of the conference] was the question of "academic freedom." . . .

In preliminary discussions . . . I could not get a satisfactory explanation of the importance of "academic freedom." I had known previously that an alderman of the city of Galesburg, irked because a college political science class was doing field research into the operations of the city government, charged at a city council meeting, that was broadcast over radio and reported in newspapers, that the study being made by the students and their professor was "subversive." The alderman further claimed that "the FBI had a list of names" of Knox professors, implying that those professors were subversive or Communists.

The accusations were easily and quickly disproved. The alderman retracted his charges and publicly apologized. Knox college issued a statement that was widely approved. It said in part:

> Knox College is keenly sensitive to the fact that communistic ideas endanger this nation. Knox College's very existence depends upon the outcome of the struggle. Knox also is aware of another danger: the growing tendency to exploit a common fear by accusations not based on fact. The fight against communism could be useless if this danger is not simultaneously recognized.
>
> Knox is confident that no member of its staff is a Communist, has communistic or other subversive sympathies, or is advocating un-American doctrines in or out of the college's classrooms. There is an obvious difference between teaching what communism is (in order that the student may know what he is fighting) and teaching that communism is desirable. The former the independent colleges must always do; the latter they cannot do and hope to survive. . . .

I had thought that the alderman's apology and the college's statement, made in November 1952, had ended the matter. . . . Yet about two weeks before I had arrived on the campus late this spring, someone had set a bomb off under the porch of the home of a college professor. . . .

When I attended a meeting of a committee of the college faculty which was trying to decide on taking some action on "academic freedom" one of the professors present . . . told me quite frankly . . . :

> You are a businessman and businessmen just can't seem to understand what academic freedom is all about. You've got to be part of the faculty to know what it means. I am afraid we would just be wasting our time trying to explain it and we would probably find ourselves getting involved in an unpleasant argument.

I pointed out to the group that perhaps the reason for so much misunderstanding about academic freedom was that faculties had not tried to explain it adequately. They apparently had come to the conclusion that, because the subject was political fireworks, they could not make others understand and consequently they had retired into their academic shells to brood about it. I expressed the opinion that if these professors could teach more complicated subjects, they certainly were able to help me understand a topic that was so important to them.

Present at the meeting was a consultant to the college. He told the group that misunderstanding by businessmen of "academic freedom," which they interpreted as a cloak to protect Communists, was seriously reducing the financial contributions of businessmen to colleges and universities. . . . Therefore . . . it was more important than ever that this question of academic freedom be cleared up, because it affected, not just the sensitive feelings of college professors, but the very future and prosperity of independent college education in this country.

Seated at the table at which we were gathered was . . . a professor, who, more than twenty-five years ago, had converted me into an enthusiastic student of history. I appealed to him for an explanation. He said:

> Academic freedom does not affect me too much. In a year or two I will retire, but academic freedom is a serious problem to these younger professors. The better ones . . . are seriously considering quitting the teaching profession. . . . They know that, as long as there is this furor over the loyalty oath and constant danger of political investigation of any statement they are likely to make in a classroom, their jobs will always be in jeopardy.

If they leave the teaching profession, less able teachers will take their places. . . . In the long run the future students of Knox and other colleges will suffer. . . .

That put the discussion on the right track. It turned out that some professors on the campus were refusing to make any public appearances before gatherings in the city of Galesburg. Though the "subversive" charges had been disproved, the suspicion remained. One professor had made a spiritual talk, entirely unrelated to politics, before a church group. When it was over a woman came up to him and asked him if he was "one of those Communists from Knox." . . .

Now there was a McCarthy in Washington and Paul W. Broyles in the Illinois state legislature. Both were demanding loyalty oaths and investigation of anyone suspected of "subversive activity," although anyone who dared to discuss communism, or suggested a study of communism or communistic literature to understand it better, or explored the role of Russia in the modern world might be suspected of subversive activity. Last year a bill, sponsored by Broyles, was passed by the Illinois legislature which called for a loyalty oath, and the appointment of a special assistant attorney general who was to investigate all suspected subversive acts or activities throughout the state of Illinois. Governor Adlai E. Stevenson vetoed the bill. . . .

In April 1953 . . . the Broyles bill was back in the Illinois state legislature. Later in June . . . I visited an old friend . . . who was a member of the legislature. The bill had passed the senate. I asked my friend how he would vote when it came before the house. He was not sure, but he was inclined to vote for it, because "we certainly don't want any Communists in our colleges." . . .

There were two factors that deeply disturbed the faculty committee at Knox as we discussed that loyalty oath. The first was that they could not maintain their intellectual honesty and sign the oath. . . . Second was that only they as teachers were suspected of disloyalty and were being separated from the rest of the population in being asked to sign a loyalty oath.

They pointed out that I would not be asked to sign a loyalty oath. I suddenly realized that I had once been in a position where

I had information that could have been dangerous to this country and yet I had not been asked to sign a loyalty oath. As the editor of a national magazine during the war, I had been told and shown "top secret" information, plans, and pictures by government officials. Many editors today surely are given similar "off the record" information to help them understand the government's plans, and yet they are not asked to sign either oaths of loyalty or secrecy. Hundreds of businessmen and thousands of designers and factory workers are manufacturing "top secret" material for the government. They are not asked to sign loyalty oaths.

But college professors who have no information that would be of value to an enemy are being asked to sign loyalty oaths simply because they might be suspect should they explore the workings of communism with their students.

My old professor at the table pointed out that Knox teachers had always been noteworthy for their independent thinking and actions. Before the Civil War they spoke openly against slavery. They were stoned and run out of Illinois towns. Were they wrong? Were they wrong now in insisting on the freedom of speech?

As a teacher of history, he was able to show that always in the development of undemocratic governments the first step was to place restrictions on teachers and to purge those who insisted on the freedom to teach. Hitler did it and so did Mussolini and also Stalin. It was done in ancient Rome. Napoleon did it, too. Even in this country, there have been instances, including Bryan's attempt to stop the teaching of evolution.

And in 1897 "the entire faculty of the Kansas Agricultural College was dismissed for their failure to subscribe to the tenets of the Populist party."

Suddenly I began to recognize the importance of the concern of these professors. . . . At the same time I realized what was wrong with the plea for "academic freedom."

While the professors were objecting to the signing of a loyalty oath because they were being separated from the rest of the population, they encouraged that separation by insisting on "academic freedom." The political rabble rousers aided them and hurt them at the same time by making "academic freedom" mean a cloak to protect the Communist sympathizers on the college campuses.

To make people understand, it was necessary to find a new term, a term that would affect all people, not just college professors. We found it. . . .

It was "intellectual freedom." "Intellectual freedom" was important to everybody. It was important to me as a businessman and a citizen because it gave me the right to discuss any subject I please, including communism, with my friends and neighbors. It would be important to me were I again an editor for it would mean that I had the right to criticize my government and its officials and to review the governments or acts of other countries. It would be important for me were I a student for it would mean I would be free to study any subject I pleased. It would be important to me were I a professor.

"Intellectual freedom" did not mean I could preach revolution and the overthrow of the government. But "intellectual freedom" did seem to embody the freedoms we know so well— the freedom of speech, the freedom of the press, the freedom of assembly, in fact it appeared to enfold in just two words the Bill of Rights of the Constitution of the United States. . . .

I realize that it was "academic freedom" that had blinded me . . . but my experience at Knox . . . indicated that academic freedom can be extremely important to the many other freedoms we love. Curtailment of any freedom, no matter how unimportant, threatens all freedoms. Let us not be blind just because a loyalty oath or restriction of a freedom does not apply to us. We cannot compromise because any threat to any phase of democracy is a threat to all of us.

DANGERS OF POLITICAL CONTROL
OF OUR COLLEGES [9]

The American educational system is protected from political control by the existence of boards of education and boards of

[9] From "Citizen and School, Freedom for Teachers," by Harold Taylor, president, Sarah Lawrence College. *Nation.* 177:265-7. October 3, 1953. Reprinted by permission.

trustees or regents. Their function is to insure that democratic means of deciding educational policies are in full operation. We are coming dangerously close to direct political control of the schools and colleges when state legislatures or Federal bodies can secure the dismissal of individual teachers on political grounds by dealing, not with the authorities responsible for appointment and dismissal, but with the teachers themselves, the books they write, and the ideas they profess.

Who, then, has the authority to control the principles and everyday practices of the American educational system? There is no single authority. The authority rests, in varying degree, in the hands of teachers, boards of education, principals, school superintendents, college presidents, parents, alumni, boards of trustees, and the voting population. It is centered in the membership of boards of trustees and boards of education, which are chartered by the state. These appoint the administrative officers, who in turn appoint the teachers. As soon as the state or Federal Government has authority to decide who should teach, what should be taught, and what should be read, the state controls the politics of American youth.

TIME FOR DECISION

EDITOR'S INTRODUCTION

In spite of the charges and counter-charges regarding the "suspect" Communist professor and his "place" in the schools, the question still before us is what to do with him and how. The Fifth Amendment controversy offers no solutions; it merely fogs the issues more than ever. The debate over whether or not academic freedom is endangered by congressional investigations hasn't presented us with any lasting or real solution, although it has added some new problems which must be given consideration.

Basically, it seems a wise procedure to pause at this point and take a careful look at the problem from the standpoint of alternatives and possible solutions. Such questions as these require an early answer:

Should the colleges cooperate and apply the recommendations of the Jenner committee to "clean their houses"? If so, what effect will this have on the future of academic freedom on the campuses of the nation? Secondly, and more important, who are the professors who should be "cleaned out" and how are they to be found?

Disregarding for the moment the arguments for or against congressional investigations, we find that the committees themselves have announced that they merely spotlight the problem, that their job was to publicize not penalize. The responsibility for action they leave to local authorities, where they contend it belongs. But again, what kind of action and how it should be administered is a problem for the future.

It seems generally conceded that Communists have no place on college faculties. But the problem of identification and definition is so great that this concession has little meaning. Senator McCarthy speaks of "Communist thinkers"; and most educators think in terms of card-carrying Communist party members. Where shall the line be drawn?

At just what point should academic freedom figure in this picture? Does the reasonable demand for effective national se-

curity measures outweigh any consideration of freedom to learn
and freedom to teach? Again, where does one draw the line
between liberty and license?

The fact that the American university is assuming a more important role in American life—thanks to extensive government
contracts in secret laboratory projects, the training of scientists
who hold the key to the atomic age, plus the education and indoctrination of the soldiers who may be called upon to fight
another Communist enemy at any moment—this calls for careful deliberation. What lasting effects will this changing character
of the American university have upon the ideal of academic freedom?

This section has been devoted to a miscellany of articles representing a number of distinct points of view. They do not
provide solutions, although they may help in clarifying some of
the questions outlined previously. This may well be a time for
decision, upon which will rest the future of academic freedom in
a society living under a constant threat of atomic war. The fears
of the academic world appear to be summed up rather completely by this reminder of Robert M. Hutchins, former president
of the University of Chicago:

> We are just emerging from an era in which a schoolteacher could
> lose her job by smoking, dancing, or using cosmetics. We should avoid
> entering one in which a professor can lose his post and his reputation
> by holding views of politics, economics, or international relations that
> are not acceptable to the majority.

It is hoped that the material in this section may offer some
clue as to the proper decision which will insure both academic
freedom in the colleges and maximum national security.

AN EVALUATION OF THE PROBLEM
OF SUBVERSIVES [1]

Have these congressional investigators any right to inquire
into the political activities and affiliations of professors? There
are those who say that these investigators should keep hands off
the colleges. . . . But it seems to me that congressional investiga-

[1] From "Dulles, Freedom, Colleges," by John B. Sheerin, C.S.P., editor of
Catholic World. Catholic World. 177:81-86. May 1953. Reprinted by permission.

tors have every right to find out if teachers have actually engaged in subversive work on or off the campus, to find out if they have been part of a conspiracy to destroy the American government. Such information would certainly be well within the scope of their function, which is to gather material that would help in the framing of legislation on a national level.

The difficult question to answer, however, is this: should the committee be empowered to inquire into the expressed views of a teacher who has not taken part in actual subversive activities? This is not easy to answer. It is not a question of firing Communists or Communist sympathizers from the faculty. Most colleges are willing to do so. The question applies only to the scope of the *Committee's* powers: should *they* have the right to ask about a teacher's political views?. . .

The congressional committees . . . have abundant evidence of communism in colleges. The question is therefore: how shall we handle this menace of communism on the campus?

There is no climate of hysteria in the United States today. There are some hysterical critics of the congressional investigators but even there, the New York *Times* . . . points out, the complaints are generally directed not against the fact of investigation but against the methods of the investigators. That there have been abuses is unquestionable. But as to a wave of hysteria among our people, let us remember that only three or four of the spies identified by Whittaker Chambers and Elizabeth Bentley have been punished. The rest are free to talk without hindrance. Judith Coplon still roams the streets of Brooklyn. No magazine or book-publisher or radio commentator is afraid to issue attacks against McCarthy, Jenner or Velde. . . .

Yet the mere fact that the investigators are not inducing hysteria in our people does not justify their attempt to quiz professors about their private political opinions. President Eisenhower believes a Communist should be expelled immediately; Senator Taft thinks he should be expelled only if he is indoctrinating his class. But what about a teacher who is not a Communist but gives a red slant to his class work?

Some will say that we should judge a man by his actions without attempting to read his intentions. Obviously, if a teacher has taken part in subversive acts he should be expelled. Moreover, if he intends to do subversive work and this intention can be discovered, there is no reason why we should wait for him to explode the bomb before expelling him from the faculty. If his teaching is of such a character that it amounts to "incitement to violence," he should be expelled.

But what of the teacher who is simply a Communist sympathizer and who gives information about communism but does not "incite to violence"? Even if the Communist party is outlawed, he could not be expelled from college on the ground of an illegal membership, as he is not a member of the party. He can be dismissed only on the ground that he is unfit to teach since as a Communist he is pledged to principles which demand that a teacher betray his trust.

I feel very doubtful about allowing a congressional committee to decide the question of a teacher's fitness to teach. That is outside the scope of the congressional investigation whose aim is to gather material helpful in the framing of national legislation. On a short visit to a college, moreover, how would the committee obtain evidence of unfitness. Observation? The teacher won't talk if he knows he is being investigated in the classroom. Information from pupils? Americans don't like the smell of a classroom spy-system, and I doubt that many students would turn "informers.". . .

A congressional committee's function should be restricted to subversive activity inquiries and to investigation of teachers "inciting to violence." If the college administration is delinquent in judging a professor's fitness to teach and stubborn in refusing to act when notified by reliable citizens, then chaos is come again. I don't think the general situation is quite as bad as that. The fundamental reality remains, that no teacher should be allowed to destroy a student's faith in the democratic charter under pretext of academic freedom. For academic freedom is not absolute or an end in itself: it means freedom to move about in the orbit of commonly accepted democratic doctrines and practices.

AN APPRAISAL OF THE "ATMOSPHERE
OF REPRESSION" [2]

No less a person than Bertrand Russell, in a communication in the *Manchester Guardian* last year, wrote . . . that a "reign of terror" exists in the United States. . . .

Mr. Russell as a visitor may not have experienced a representative side of American life. But what shall we say of the following remark of Mr. Robert M. Hutchins: "Everywhere in the United States, university professors, whether or not they have tenure, are silenced by the general atmosphere of repression that now prevails.". . . And this at a time when professors have actually been more outspoken than ever in the past against arbitrary actions by university and state authorities. . . . College professors . . . today as a group . . . are as intellectually bold as any profession in the nation. Although criticism and attacks on schools and teachers have come from all quarters, professors are giving an excellent account of themselves in rejoinder and counter-attack.

Now and again, other individuals, some even in official posts, take up Mr. Hutchins's cry and assert that American college teachers are petrified with fear, unwilling to discuss controversial issues or to protest measures of which they disapprove. Many different things are here confused. It is true that the number of criticisms and attacks on the schools has increased and, here and there, some fantastic things have occurred. . . . But it is just as true that college teachers have never fought back so unitedly, spiritedly and successfully as today. They won on the key point in the University of California case; they helped put to rout the House on Un-American Activities when it sought to check on textbooks; they are slowly turning the tide against loyalty oaths; they have condemned investigations by congressional committees often and vigorously.

To circulate the myth that "everywhere in the United States, university professors" have been cowed or silenced by Senators McCarthy and McCarran or whoever else is identified with the

[2] From "Freedom in American Culture," by Sidney Hook, chairman of the graduate department of philosophy, New York University, noted author. *New Leader*. section 2:s 1-s 15. April 6, 1953. Reprinted by permission.

spirit of repression is not only to circulate an untruth but may, if given credence, actually contribute to bringing about such a state of affairs. It is to discourage teachers from continuing their role as active defenders of academic freedom. My own impression is that teachers today are more aroused and more active in behalf of academic freedom than they have ever been in my thirty-five years of experience as college student and teacher. . . .

Some months ago, a professional liberal figure appeared on a television program on the state of civil liberties in America. At a moment when the cameras brought him so close that one could almost look down his throat, he was shouting: "It's getting so that a man can't open his mouth in this country." Whether the millions of people who got a glimpse of his tonsils appreciated the irony of the situation is doubtful. . . .

The truth of the matter is that many American men and women of good will, and large sections of American liberalism, particularly in the universities, are much less concerned with the outrages of Communist totalitarianism against their victims, and the threats to their own freedom in the extension of the Kremlin's power, than they were with the outrages of Fascist totalitarianism, and the threats of a victory by Hitler. Who does not remember the ferment and stir on American campuses from 1933 to 1939 even before the worst iniquities of Hitlerism were known? The committees, the meetings, the mass demonstrations and picketings, the pamphlets and leaflets against fascism were almost an everyday occurrence. Anyone who suggested that we should try to understand the Nazis despite their distasteful foreign policy, that we should send ambassadors of good will, build cultural bridges, would have been shouted down. Had he said that all the excitement about nazism and fascism was a form of hysteria because, after all, Hitler had so few followers in this country, and those mostly cranks and comic-opera figures, he would have been considered a Nazi apologist.

If we match Hitler's first six years with the six years that have elapsed since the end of World War II, we find that Stalin has absorbed more countries, killed more people, extirpated more democratic institutions more thoroughly than even the psychotic barbarian, Hitler. Where is the excitement, the moral indignation, the impassioned protest? In 1935, I could rouse the academic community to Hitler's latest decree or to the attempt of some Polish universities to make Jewish students sit on yellow benches. In 1948, when I sought to organize a protest against the coldblooded execution of Czech students after the Communist *coup d'état,* I could hardly raise a corporal's guard in addition to members of the old Committee for Cultural Freedom and their friends. The stalwarts who shouted against Hitler, against Dollfuss, against Mussolini, Franco, Chiang Kai-shek, Pilsudski, Metaxas, were silent before the bloody events in Latvia, Estonia, Lithuania, Poland, Rumania, Bulgaria, Czechoslovakia, Greece and East Germany which not only destroyed every vestige of academic freedom but took the lives of thousands of democratic students and professors. I could rouse them with a resolution or a meeting of protest against Argentina. But although these individuals are certainly *not* Communists, they are apathetic or cynical to the global Communist threat. They are still convinced that our liberties are in greater danger from American fascism than from any other source; they still fail to see that one can distinguish, but cannot separate, the American Communist movement from the Soviet world conspiracy against the United States. They do not see the *international* character of the Communist attack against the free institutions of the world evidenced in large things as well as small like the Kremlin's willingness to exchange a British citizen in Hungary for a Communist partisan in Malaya, and its frightening successes in picturing the atomic spies, the Rosenbergs, as innocent victims of American "terror."

So long as this remains true and American liberals do not take the leadership in the struggle against communism, wherever it is an issue, they create the conditions in which demagogues thrive who oppose communism and liberalism both. It is only under such liberal leadership that peace may be won without appeasement and, if it comes to a struggle, democratic institutions and the rights of heresy preserved.

A LIBERAL'S DEFENSE OF SCHOOL PROBES [3]

Like most thoughtful Americans, I shudder at the prospect of an investigation of schools and colleges by men of the character of Senators McCarthy and Jenner, using the methods they habitually employ. Much unnecessary damage has already been done to the teaching profession—itself not exceptional for outspoken courage—by special loyalty oaths and various forms of ill-considered, witch-hunting, legislation.

The opposition to this sort of business among friends of civil liberties is admirable in spirit. I gladly associate myself with it. But good people, when they let emotion run away with logic and tie up the rights of honest dissenters and non-conformers with the right of Fascist and Communist conspirators to teach the children of democracy, hand over to the McCarthys a powerful weapon to use against the freedom that they want to serve.

The sin of the Communist, or Fascist, or Ku Klux Klaner, which should bar him from teaching in our schools, is not his unconventional opinion on political and economic matters, openly and honestly avowed. Against faulty opinions society can protect itself by argument and by enforcing accepted rules forbidding political or sectarian indoctrination in the classrooms of our public schools.

But society has no such defense against conspiracy; against the exaltation of bad faith into virtue; against obedience to the terrible chief commandment of communism, "You shall believe and do whatsoever the party bids you to advance its interests." He who gives his allegiance to this sort of organization signs away his conscience. Stalin's opinion on philosophy, religion, music, biology, history, economics and politics becomes his creed, and to defend slave camps and purges his duty. The right of the Communist to teach should be denied because he has given away his freedom in the quest for truth. And that is fundamental to democracy.

[3] From "School Probe Upheld," letter to the editor by Norman Thomas, Socialist party leader, writer, and lecturer, and chairman of the Post War World Council. New York *Times*. p E 8. February 8, 1953. Reprinted by permission.

Yet good people argue emotionally that academic freedom is lost if in these anxious days a teacher is asked by legitimate authority if he is a Communist, or if, his allegiance to Communists being acknowledged or proved, he is denied the right to teach.

Men who claim to recognize communism for what it is argue that we must not impute guilt to the Communist teacher by association; that the chances are that he will not obey a party order to betray his country; that pupils and society are sufficiently protected by the rule that the teacher may be disciplined for proved unprofessional conduct; that the Constitution somehow guarantees to teachers the right to silence on their deepest convictions.

To all of these contentions there are simple answers. The teacher who surrenders his conscience to a conspiratorial party is guilty of more than guilt by association. In years gone by the teacher may have acted in misapprehension of the nature of communism. If so, he is certainly entitled to forgiveness and the confidence of society. But he who today persists in Communist allegiance is either too foolish or too disloyal to democratic ideals to be allowed to teach in our schools.

The constitutional guarantees which properly apply to criminal proceedings do not apply to protect the right to employment in "sensitive" positions—among which is a teacher's post. The right to stay out of jail is not a right to employment. No man should be found guilty of a crime if there is reasonable doubt, but no man should be employed in a sensitive position if there is reasonable doubt of his loyalty or trustworthiness.

He is a poor teacher who can't considerably indoctrinate pupils with whom he is all day long without being caught in a specific act. And he is a cowardly teacher who is unwilling to avow his deep convictions and justify his right to hold them. It is indeed difficult to keep our McCarthys from deliberately confusing dissent with conspiracy and from abusing legitimate rights of inquiry. It will be more easily done if champions of liberty recognize communism for what it is and abandon the attempt to protect honest men by putting practitioners of Communist lies and deceit upon the same level of right.

RESTORATION OF FAITH IN
AMERICAN COLLEGES [4]

Over the last five years, the American people have been losing their confidence in American education. Where they were once fountains of pride, universities are now sources of suspicion, even to some of their own alumni. Where before, they were subject to only routine governmental surveillance, both public and private schools have become legislative punching bags; cursed at, investigated, and legislated against with monotonous frequency. Even the concept "academic freedom," formerly considered as vital to a university as football and ivy, is in bad repute. Like "peace" and "democracy," academic freedom has gone the way of terms discredited through use by the nation's enemies.

This sudden disillusionment is rooted in a popular conviction that universities have been and are now breeding grounds for communism. . . .

The exasperating thing about this attitude is its persistence despite the undeniable contributions universities continue to make to the national welfare and security. . . . More top-secret research, more trained leadership for government and industry are flowing out of universities now than at any other time, and yet the public insists on drawing its impressions not from the river of loyalty but from the trickle of Communist affiliation.

This mass delusion does not . . . stem from a chronic public distaste for intellectuality. It is the outlet for frustrations born of war and preparation for war. It is the kind of scapegoat-flogging that almost inevitably results from seemingly endless international tension. In American education, the public has found reflections of communism it can attack more safely and successfully than those in the distant and powerful Soviet state. It matters not that the very vulnerability of "red professors" is an indication of the irrelevance to the total scheme of Soviet conspiracy. A "red" is a "red," in the public mind, whether he is killing Americans in Korea or dodging congressional questions

[4] From "Universities and the Public Trust: an Editorial." *Harvard Crimson,* Fifth Annual Academic Freedom Report. p M-12. June 10, 1953. Reprinted by permission.

in Washington. The desire for a scapegoat makes events of the thirties just as appalling as those of the fifties. It turns liberals into Communists, and past party members into present. It obliterates recollection of the public's own attitude toward Russia during the war years. For where there is hysteria, there can be no room for distinctions. . . . You can call the Veldes and Jenners whatever you like . . . but the volume of their fan mail testifies to the faithfulness with which they represent and satisfy public opinion. . . .

There are many good, honest Republicans who, even though they realize how the present hysteria distorts the real contributions of universities, hesitate to speak up against it. Noticing that the only men, books and ideas presently being purged are those they have opposed in social politics since the New Deal, they privately thank investigators for devastating their political opponents. Unfortunately, they underestimate the awful appetite of the scapegoat desire. They might look back at the French Revolution, when purger followed purged to the guillotine, or over to Massachusetts, where the "reds-in-education" issue is the stick Democrats use to beat Republicans. By blandly assuming the attack on academic freedom can stop before it reaches their own ideas, nonliberals show not only intolerance, but ignorance of the nature of the danger.

To correct the public attitude without sacrificing academic freedom will be no easy job for American education. It will require, on the part of every person involved in education—student, teacher, administrator, alumnus—the realization that they must fight for the privileges they could formerly take for granted. It will require the very ability to distinguish unorthodoxy from totalitarianism that the general public does not have.

Teachers and students will have to realize that entire academic communities are being judged by the things they do. They can no longer, if they wish education to regain popular respect, indulge in intellectual luxuries such as joining groups without asking of their real purpose. When called before investigating committees, they must realize the reputation of their college sits on the stand with them, and they should answer all questions but those which they know will lead to criminal or perjury charges. Although silence may save friends or express moral indignation, it unquestionably tacitly incriminates their entire university community in the eyes of the public. Reacting in this way to investigations, teachers then equally owe it to their institutions not to let their temporary unpopularity prevent them from honest pursuit of the truth and full use of their political rights as citizens.

But teachers and students cannot be expected to act this way unless they know that college officials, that group in education most prone to compromise academic freedom in the past, will stand behind them. Our universities have a responsibility to the public and themselves to expel teachers who have broken the law, or whose totaliarian beliefs so twist their teaching and research to render them unfit for their profession. But they have an equal responsibility to make sure the implication of unfitness that springs from use of the Fifth Amendment, membership in subversive groups, or any other indirect evidence is backed up by fact before any teacher is disciplined. In this way, mutual trust between universities and their faculties can be restored.

But defenses of education are hollow if they issue only from within university walls. In the long run, the only effective antidote to this distrust lies in elements of the public itself. Let respected citizens—trustees of universities and others whose loyalty is unquestioned—speak up in defense of universities. Let them cast their defenses in the same terms of anti-communism as the attacks have been. For the anti-Communist record of American universities is a long and proud one, needing only respected advocates and full publicity. If these tangible fruits of academic freedom become as much a part of the public consciousness as the case against it, the mutual trust between universities and the public can once more be restored.

THE DILEMMA OF ADMINISTRATIVE RESPONSIBILITY [5]

Communists should not be appointed to any position in a school, college, or university. . . . *Known Communists* should be dismissed. But . . . the independence of each college and uni-

[5] From "Freedom of the Mind," an address before the American Association of School Administrators in Atlantic City, N.J., February 17, 1953, by Mrs. Agnes E. Meyer, wife of Eugene Meyer, board chairman, Washington *Post*. *National Education Association News*. 7:1-8. February 27, 1953. Reprinted by permission.

versity would be threatened if governmental agencies of any sort should start inquiries into the nature of the instruction given, for their independence as corporate, scholarly organizations is of supreme importance.

How, then, should the universities decide who is a "known Communist" and how to handle the problem? If a university president decides that a serious allegation of communism against one of his faculty members deserves attention, he should set up a committee of inquiry made up of academic colleagues, possibly with legal advisers to assist them. The president must show respect for his faculty by refusing to search into possible subversives on his own motion. He assumes the loyalty of all scholars until factual proof to the contrary comes to his attention. Only then does he act—and he acts only to have the scholar's colleagues determine whether he is a Communist. If the accusations against him in the judgment of his fellows seem to be well founded, he should be asked to resign, since he has joined a conspiratorial group hostile to the central aim of all universities —the search for truth. . . .

The relationship in our country of government to education has never been thoroughly explored. Not only has this relationship never been spelled out, but the relation of many university boards of trustees to their faculties has not been clearly defined. Some of our oldest colleges and universities have established clear-cut policies of tenure; others have dismissed faculty members in the most authoritarian manner when they professed ideas which the trustees disliked. Similar highhanded dismissals of public-school teachers by their boards of education have also taken place. As a result, the universities and the public-school system are now in a precarious position, lacking clearly defined safeguards, and, therefore, exposed to the demands of any pressure group with selfish economic interests to protect or with ideological nostrums to preach. In other words, our tradition of academic freedom is not firmly grounded and our whole educational system may be brought under government control unless we manage to clarify the role of our free universities in the national scene, of the public schools in the community, and the reasons why academic security and academic freedom are the foundation of civil freedom itself. . . .

Both our institutions of higher learning and our public schools must strengthen their own situations if the congressional threats to academic freedom are to be resisted successfully. . . .

But the solution . . . is largely dependent upon the way the colleges and universities, both public and private, face the weaknesses in their own organizations. To highlight the unhappy position in which higher education finds itself in our country, let me compare it with that of the European universities. For such an outrageous challenge as some congressmen have flung in the face of our college faculties, presidents and trustees, could not possibly take place in England. Oxford and Cambridge are supported by state funds. Yet no member of the British Parliament would dare interfere with their academic freedom. Why not? Because the English universities are democratic, independent, self-governing groups of scholars. It is the faculty which runs the university. The faculty *is* the university. They have no boards of trustees, no alumni secretaries, no presidents or other administrative officials who have power over the faculty. That is why academic freedom in England is unassailable to political adventurers.

What is the typical practice in our country? I quote a report of the American Association of University Professors: "In the typical (American) institution in 1941 the board of trustees appointed the deans, and the deans, in turn, designated the department executives, all without benefit of consultation, with the teaching staff." In many of our smaller colleges the faculty have been considered little more than hired hands.

This undemocratic situation in many of our institutions of learning has confused the whole problem of academic freedom. . . . If academic freedom is to be put on a sound basis . . . all university and college trustees must study their relation to their faculties and make a clear division between the professional responsibilities of the faculty and the lay responsibilities of the trustees.

But since this cannot be achieved overnight, the trustees of our colleges and universities must realize in the face of Mc-

Carthy's threats more strongly than ever before that they are not only the trustees of a lot of buildings and grounds but of a sacred tradition—freedom of learning, freedom of expression and freedom of the mind. It is the trustees in the first place who must now accept the onus of their position and tell all the congressional investigators that they themselves are responsible for the selection of the presidents or deans who in turn select the faculty and that, if anybody in their institution has to answer his questions, they must be the ones to do so. In fact our university officials had better come forward and accept this responsibility voluntarily for otherwise they will be forced to do so. For McCarthy has said that he is not only going to expose "communistic thinkers" wherever he finds them but the people who appointed them to their jobs. That will involve any or all university presidents and trustees.

SECURITY AND FREEDOM [6]

Membership on the faculty of a college or university is a privilege—not a right; a privilege that ought not to be given to a Communist under any circumstances. The central idea of the American way of life is personal freedom. One essential characteristic of an American college or university is the freedom of the faculty to seek the truth and to publicize and teach it. The Communist is not free to seek the truth nor to teach it. By his membership in the party he has surrendered his freedom politically, economically, and morally. There have been, and probably still are, those who have held that mere membership in the Communist party should not, by itself, constitute a basis for refusal to appoint any individual to a college faculty, or to dismiss him if already appointed. This view suggests that Communists should be rejected or dismissed only when there is evidence that they are using their positions to propagandize their Communist ideology. I reject this view. It is to me a most naïve disregard of the facts with respect to membership in the party. There

[6] From a speech by A. Blair Knapp, president of Denison University, Granville, Ohio. *At Denison*, monthly publication of Denison University. 13:1-3. March 1953. Reprinted by permission. (Also in *Congressional Record*. 99:A1229. March 9, 1953.)

might have been some justification of this view some years ago when we knew much less about the party than we now know. It no longer can be justified. Those who still proclaim this view, in my opinion, are doing the teaching profession great harm. They are distorting the true meaning of academic freedom and making it suspect in the eyes of many who should be defending it vigorously as an essential characteristic of our colleges and universities. The air would be cleared and truer perspective created if those who are professionally engaged in higher education, either as teachers, administrators, or researchers, would let it be understood that Communists cannot be professionally acceptable. . . .

The responsibility of seeing to it that Communists are denied the privilege of faculty status rests squarely on the administrative leaders of each college or university. . . . If we who are responsible for the administration of colleges and universities fail to exercise proper care in meeting this responsibility, we invite the disorder, the confusion, and the injury to education generally which comes from the investigations by government committees. If we would keep our own houses in order, we would not have to pay this price.

THE COMING POLITICAL STRUGGLE [7]

The present controversy between academic freedom, on one hand, and loyalty oaths and congressional investigations, on the other is, unescapedly, a matter of politics. It is political because under our system of government we must resort either to the courts or to the lawmakers for the final resolution of an issue. The Supreme Court of the United States has followed numerous rulings by state courts in holding that a state does have the right to set up qualifications for teachers and that disqualifications may include association through membership in organizations held to be subversive and disloyal. Since the courts have ruled, the next resort is to the lawmakers, which brings us back to the people

[7] From "Academic Freedom and Politics," by Walton Manning, graduate student, School of Education, Indiana University. *Phi Delta Kappan.* 24:398-400. June 1953. Reprinted by permission.

who elect them, and to issues which can be settled only at the ballot box.

Many college and university teachers have declared personally and through their organizations that they oppose loyalty oaths and investigations as breaches in the walls of academic freedom. In this, they are taking a political stand and one which in many instances is a partisan political position. . . .

Two factors are discernible in the present controversy. One, the issue of communism, has been widely identified, and in many states the fight over this issue has been resolved. The second issue, however, lies ahead, and it will stir up increasing controversy in the next few years. This issue involves the right of a teacher to engage in teaching which tends to lead to an acceptance of socialism—not socialism of the Soviet Union variety, but socialism based on a democratic framework such as that found in some European countries and called by many "Fabian" socialism.

It is unfortunate, but seemingly true, that the very fact that university teachers are fighting the Communist issue will provide the ammunition and impetus to those now planning the next phase of the fight, which will be against socialism of any variety. This idea is indeed difficult for many teachers to understand, much less accept. For twenty years, teachers watched this nation march step after step toward centralization of government through enactment of laws in areas previously left to the states. . . . Now they face an administration which knows that it came to power largely because of a swing of the people *away* from centralization. . . .

The courts have ruled that one's *beliefs* can be a consideration of qualification and . . . a new scrutiny of beliefs in colleges is under way. Many informed people think, further, that the major emphasis of this scrutiny evolves around the right of those who believe in socialism and those who actively teach anti-Christian doctrines to continue to teach in publicly supported colleges and universities. That this will become a partisan political issue on a national scale few can doubt. . . .

That the struggle will be bitter is practically certain. The power and the present temper of the people is on the side of the enemies of socialism . . . and modern education is far more vulnerable to a charge of socialism and non-Christianity than it is to charges of communism. Many educational writings are either openly socialistic or sympathetic, and many intelligent men and women honestly believe that democratic goals cannot be achieved except by the adoption of democratic socialism. . . .

Those who will ignite the battle against socialism will represent a force and a fury which will surprise many intellectuals. There is in this nation, in spite of apparent contradictions, a deep faith in a system of competition which pays more for better work. There is also, in America, a great unwillingness to replace faith in Christianity with faith in man. These people view the Bible and the Constitution as the foundations of freedom. To defend this creed, to pass it on with firmer faith and conviction to their children, millions of Americans will devote their lives and their fortunes. Those who challenge this creed may be forced to acknowledge the strength of an American faith that transcends the right of any individual to trample it while enjoying its benefits.

NEED FOR NON-APPEASEMENT [8]

Since the founding of our Republic, it has always been feared by some that freedom of speech—utterances critical of our government, our Congress, or our elected officials—constitute a challenge to the established order and are inherently dangerous. With the full knowledge that free speech might jeopardize established credos and the generally accepted order of things as they are, the framers of our Constitution wrote into the basic law of our land the First Amendment. They did so in the conviction that suppression of thought, of speech, of the press, and of public assembly, would be even more dangerous to the whole concept of a free democratic society.

The alarming tendency today to abrogate the First Amendment in the name of patriotism finds an easy and vulnerable tar-

[8] From "University Must Stand Firm Against Attacks on Liberty," by Senator Thomas C. Hennings, Jr. (Democrat, Missouri). *Washington University Student Life.* 74:18+. February 20, 1953. Reprinted by permission. (Also in the *Congressional Record.* 99:A1211. March 9, 1953.)

get in all of our institutions of learning. Any institution which is willing to place a straitjacket on academic freedom to demand rigid conformity from its teachers, and to content itself with dead-level uniformity in the indoctrination of its students, will probably escape the slings and arrows of congressional committees and of sometimes misguided patriotic organizations. It may continue to be the recipient of substantial endowments and to enroll new students. A foundation which places such restraints on academic freedom . . . will, by the same token, have acknowledged its surrender to the cult of mental regimentation which is gaining a dismaying popularity in some quarters. . . .

A true American university cannot ignobly debase itself by restricting learning for fear of reprisals and loss of endowments, but in proclaiming the right of dissent, it must scorn the consequences. Where education is shackled and the right of dissent denied, the spirit of liberty is dammed at its fountainhead. I do not minimize the fact that it will take a good deal of fortitude on the part of the colleges and universities to stand firm against attacks on academic freedom, for it will come from many quarters and in various guises. The temper of our times, sadly, indicates that there will be continued charges of subversive influences on the campuses, demands for loyalty oaths, condemnation of textbooks which may, in the opinion of some, contain heretical ideas.

THE PROBLEM OF "PROFESSOR X" [9]

A university president's mail is an amazing daily grist of assorted pressures and problems. . . . Today, however, in the fear of communism, and with more and more investigating committees, the mails are flooded with letters from alumni and other friends challenging the President "to do something about Professor X." . . .

It is clear, so it is vigorously argued, that he is harmful to the public relations of the university. It is reported that he is costing countless thousands in diverted gifts and bequests, while

[9] From "The Red Probes and Professor X," by Deane W. Malott, president, Cornell University. New York *Herald Tribune*. p5. June 21, 1953. Reprinted by permission. (Also in *Congressional Record*. 99:A4711. July 18, 1953.)

prospective students are alleged to be selecting other and more conservative institutions. Some university trustees fret and worry over the expression of any idea inconsistent with the philosophy of William McKinley.

Why not do something about Professor X? But what?

Should those who in this unstable day voice dissent be classed as enemies of society? Are all who depart from the ranks of the so-called conservatives to be muffled or fired? If so by whom, and judged by what standards?

I am not a social scientist, but from my own conservative point of view I have an uneasy feeling that the American way of life, the freedom which we all hold so dear, cannot and will not return to the simple "free enterprise" of our Founding Fathers. Our problem rather is to preserve as much freedom, as much initiative, as much self-reliance as we possibly can in view of our present state of society, our material standards of living, our burgeoning population, and our international responsibilities.

Our only hope, then, is to preserve free speech, the right of independent thought, the right of dissent, without danger of being cast into the gloomy framework of treachery or evil intentions. I am not really concerned about Professor X, singly or in his relatively small group. He may be addled, he may be unwise in his utterances, he may be dangerous in a limited way and in limited scope. He certainly may be wrong in his beliefs.

But who is to say? Heretics have been persecuted throughout history. Truth somehow prevails. We cannot be fearless in the face of truth yet fear the effect of heresy.

From investigation, incrimination, and attack, a miserable dissenter may here and there be brought to heel. There may be tracked down a few professors, who, in the early forties, espoused some aspects of the Russian cause.

But these investigations may go to such lengths that professors out adventuring on the frontiers of the social sciences, or in any other discipline, will fear to express themselves; they will succumb to the temptation to play it safe, else in some unforeseen day, in another framework of social and political attitudes, their words may be used to the detriment of their careers.

The teaching profession must not be driven from its traditional stronghold of free speech to a position where it will fear to stand up and be counted. With academic tenure goes the responsibility for a clear and forthright definition of one's view. These professors of ours must have the right to profess; they must not be scourged from the public forum, else eventually only conformists will enter the teaching profession, leadership in the realm of ideas will wane, and the universities will sink to mediocrity.

Thinking citizens must stand behind the principles of freedom of thought and of expression. Implicit is the freedom to make mistakes, to search through error for truth, to express postulates which have not common acceptance.

Academic freedom cannot be preserved by academicians making speeches to each other. It must be maintained by the will of the American people who trust their universities as the citizens of this Republic have always trusted, and relied upon, education as a basic tenet of our American culture.

We might remember that there are no nonconformists in the totalitarian segments of the modern world.

BIBLIOGRAPHY

An asterisk (*) preceding a reference indicates that the article or a part of it has been reprinted in this book.

BOOKS, PAMPHLETS, AND DOCUMENTS

Barrett, E. L. Jr. Tenney committee: legislative investigation of subversive activities in California. 400p. Cornell University Press. Ithaca, N.Y. '51.

Barth, Alan. Loyalty of free men. 253p. Viking Press. New York. '51.

Biddle, Francis. Fear of freedom. 263p. Doubleday & Co. New York. '52.

Buckley, W. F. Jr. God and man at Yale: the superstitions of "academic freedom." 240p. Regnery. Chicago. '51.

California. Senate. Opposition to loyalty; eleventh report. 201p. The Senate. Sacramento, Calif. '53.

Carr, R. K. House committee on un-American activities, 1945-50. 489p. Cornell University Press. Ithaca, N.Y. '53.

*Chamberlain, L. H. Loyalty and legislative action. 254p. Cornell University Press. Ithaca, N.Y. '51.

Conant, J. B. Education and liberty. 160p. Harvard University Press. Cambridge, Mass. '53.

Countryman, Vern. Un-American activities in the state of Washington: the work of the Canwell committee. 405p. Cornell University Press. Ithaca, N.Y. '51.

*Gellhorn, Walter, ed. States and subversion. 454p. Cornell University Press. Ithaca, N.Y. '52.

Hullfish, H. G. ed. Educational freedom in an age of anxiety. 229p. Harper & Bros. New York. '53.

Hutchins, R. M. Conflict in education. 112p. Harper and Bros. New York. '53.

Jones, H. M. ed. Primer of intellectual freedom. 191p. Harvard University Press. Cambridge, Mass. '49.

*Kostka, William. Academic freedom opened my eyes. 9p. The author. Denver, Colo. '53.

Melby, E. O., and Puner, Morton, eds. Freedom and public education. 314p. Frederick A. Praeger. New York. '53.

New Jersey. Committee to Investigate Communistic and Un-American Teachings and Activities in the Public Schools and Tax-supported Colleges and Universities in the State of New Jersey. Report to Governor Alfred E. Driscoll. 16p. Trenton, N.J. '53.

*Newsweek Club and Educational Bureaus. New crisis for education. (Platform study guide) 19p. The Bureaus. 152 W. 42d St. New York 18. '52.

*Oregon. System of Higher Education. Oath or affirmation of allegiance (as required in Chapter 115, Laws of Oregon 1921). Salem. n.d.

Sanford, C. W. and others, eds. Schools and national security. 292p. McGraw-Hill Book Co. New York. '53.

Stewart, G. R. Year of the oath. 154p. Doubleday & Co. New York. '50.

*Stewart, M. S. Loyalty in a democracy. (Public Affairs Pamphlet no 179) 32p. Public Affairs Committee. New York. '52.

Ulman, Ruth, ed. University Debaters' Annual, 1950-1951. 256p. H. W. Wilson Co. New York. '51.
    Loyalty oaths in colleges. p 122-54.

*United States. Congress. United States Code, 1946 edition, supplement IV. Supt. of Docs. Washington 25, D.C. '50.
    Text of the Internal Security Act of 1950, Title I—Subversive Activities Control Act of 1950.

United States. House of Representatives. Permit Communist conspirators to be teachers? study by H. A. Long. (H. Doc. no213) 47p. 83d Congress, 1st session. Supt. of Docs. Washington 25, D.C. '53.

United States. House of Representatives. Un-American Activities Committee. Communist methods of infiltration (education); hearings, February 25-April 27, 1953. 436p. 83d Congress, 1st session. The Committee. Washington, D.C. '53.

United States. Senate. Judiciary Committee. Subversive influence in the educational process; hearings, September 8-October 13, 1952, before the subcommittee to investigate the administration of the internal security act and other internal security laws. 412p. 82d Congress, 2d session. Supt. of Docs. Washington 25, D.C. '52.

*United States. Senate. Judiciary Committee. Subversive influence in the educational process; hearings, February 10-May 21, 1953, before the subcommittee to investigate the administration of the internal security act and other internal security laws. 1006p. 83d Congress, 1st session. The Committee. Washington, D.C. '53.

*United States. Senate. Judiciary Committee. Subversive influence in the educational process; report of the subcommittee to investigate the administration of the internal security act and other internal security laws, January 2, 1952. 13p. 82d Congress, 2d session. The Committee. Washington, D.C. '52.

*United States. Senate. Judiciary Committee. Subversive influence in the educational process; report of the subcommittee to investigate the administration of the internal security act and other internal security laws, July 17, 1953. 36p. 83d Congress, 1st session. The Committee. Washington, D. C. '53.

*University of Washington. Communism and academic freedom; record of the tenure cases at the University of Washington. 125p. University of Washington Press. Seattle. '49.

*Wagner, K. L. Statement [on Oregon loyalty oath]. 1p. mimeo. American Legion. Department of Oregon. 702 General George A. White Building. Portland 4. n.d.
Press release.

*Wilcox, Clair, ed. Civil liberties under attack. 155p. University of Pennsylvania Press. Philadelphia. '51.

PERIODICALS

America. 88:614. Mr. 7, '53. Furor over witch hunts. A. E. Meyer.

America. 89:77-8. Ap. 18, '53. Commies and academic freedom. R. C. Hartnett.

American Association of University Professors Bulletin. 36:225-36. Summer '50. Academic freedom—German origin and American development. L. L. Rockwell.

American Association of University Professors Bulletin. 36:629-45. Winter '50. Rationale of academic freedom. Dr. Scott.

American Association of University Professors Bulletin. 38:10-25. Spring '52. Teaching of intellectual freedom. Alexander Meiklejohn.

American Association of University Professors Bulletin. 38:402-12. Autumn '52. Liberty and the pursuit of truth. J. E. Baker.

American Association of University Professors Bulletin. 38:517-19. Winter '52. Academic independence. J. B. Conant.

American Association of University Professors Bulletin. 38:520-7. Winter '52. Freedom and the humanities. Learned Hand.

*American Association of University Professors Bulletin. 39:5-15. Spring '53. Universities and political authority. Alan Barth.

*American Association of University Professors Bulletin. 39:93-4. Spring '53. Resolutions adopted by the American Association of University Professors at its 39th annual meeting.

*American Association of University Professors Bulletin. 39:122-3. Spring '53. 1940 statement of principles on academic freedom and tenure of the American Association of University Professors.

American Forum of the Air. 16, no 15:1-10. Ap. 12, '53. How should academic freedom be assured? Karl Mundt and others.

American Magazine. 153:108-12. F. '52. What a loyalty test really is. Clarence Woodbury.

American Mercury. 74:29-37. Mr. '52. Colossal flunk. W. F. Buckley, Jr.

American Mercury. 75:37-43. N. '52. What is guilt by association? Sidney Hook.

American Mercury. 76:22-3. Ja. '53. Is freedom of expression really threatened? Eugene Lyons.

*American Mercury. 76:111-44. My. '53. Communism and the colleges. J. B. Matthews.

*American Mercury. 76:101-7. Je. '53. Freedom to agree. W. F. Buckley, Jr.

American Mercury. 77:70-3. N. '53. College students look at academic freedom. Robert Munger.

American Scholar. 22:393-8. Autumn '53. Loyalty and freedom. Archibald MacLeish.

American School Board Journal. 127:31-2. N. '53. Teachers' loyalty oaths in the courts: upheld. B. A. Hess.

Annals of the American Academy of Political and Social Science. 280: 133-41. Mr. '52. Colleges, ethics, and the public. R. E. Himstead.

*Antioch Review. 12:195-202. Summer '52. Swearing to one's loyalty. Nanette Dembitz.

Association of American Colleges Bulletin. 39:103. Mr. '53. Report of the Commission on Academic Freedom and Academic Tenure. E. S. Briggs.

Association of American Colleges Bulletin. 39:377-83. O. '53. Colleges and communism. C. H. Marvin.

*At Denison (monthly newsletter from Denison University). 13:1-3. Mr. '53. Security and freedom. A. B. Knapp.

*Atlantic Monthly. 191:36-40. Je. '53. How much academic freedom? H. M. Jones.

Atlantic Monthly. 191:41-3. Je. '53. What is academic freedom? Joseph Alsop.

Brown Alumni Monthly. 43:4-6. Mr. '53. That freedom may endure. H. M. Wriston.

Bulletin of the Atomic Scientists. 9:2. F. '53. Scientists defend themselves on loyalty charges.

Bulletin of the Atomic Scientists. 9:16+. F. '53. Some thoughts on loyalty; excerpt from an address delivered at the University of Chicago Law School Alumni Association Annual Dinner, November 21, 1951. A. E. Stevenson.

Bulletin of the Atomic Scientists. 9:23-5. F. '53. Professor and his public. J. H. Hildebrand.

Bulletin of the Atomic Scientists. 9:176-86+. Je. '53. Invoking the fifth amendment. Bernard Meltzer and Harry Kolver, Jr.

Bulletin of the Atomic Scientists. 9:187. Je. '53. Rights and responsibilities of universities. A. Simpson.

*Bulletin of the Atomic Scientists. 9:193-4. Je. '53. Integrity of the universities—how to defend it. Alexander Meiklejohn.

Business Week. p200. Mr. 28, '53. Freedom to teach.

*Catholic World. 177:81-5. My. '53. Dulles, freedom, colleges. J. B. Sheerin.

Changing Times. p23-4. N. '52. Do colleges breed Communists? Douglas McGregor.

*Christian Science Monitor. p4. Je. 15, '53. Schools in midwest defend freedom of inquiry—even into communism.

Civil Liberties. 109:2. F. '53. Oklahoma oath.

*Colorado Alumnus. 43:30. Je. '53. From where we're sitting, editorial.

Colorado Alumnus. 43:30-1. Je. '53. Academic freedom—our split personality. R. J. Blakely.

Columbia Law Review. 51:587-604. My. '51. Defense of public education from subversion. James Marshall.

Columbia Law Review. 51:606-59. My. '51. Internal security act of 1950. (By the editors of the Columbia Law Review.)

*Commentary. 15:537-46. Je. '53. Do silent witnesses defend civil liberties? A. F. Westin.

Commercial and Financial Chronicle. 177:2185+. My. 21, '53. On academic freedom. William Chamberlain.

Commonweal. 56:601. S. 26, '52. Subversion in our schools.

Commonweal. 57:319. Ja. 2, '53. Loyalty by oath.

Commonweal. 57:400. Ja. 23, '53. Fear and freedom; letter to faculty of Hunter College. G. N. Shuster.

Commonweal. 58:11-13. Ap. 10, '53. Academic freedom. G. N. Shuster.

*Congressional Record. 99:1378. F. 20, '53. Remarks before the Senate. Wayne Morse.

*Congressional Record. 99:A4721-2. Jl. 18, '53. Address by Lewis K. Gough, past commander of the American Legion.

Counterattack (weekly newsletter issued by American Business Consultants). Mr. 6, '53.

*Editorial Research Reports. 1, no6:103-19. F. 11, '53. Red teachers and educational freedom. H. B. Shaffer.

Education. 72:337-40. Ja. '52. Education's function in a democracy. R. G. Newman.

Educational Record. 34:5-16. Ja. '53. Freedom of the mind and American higher education. J. L. Mathershead, Jr.

Educational Record. 34:154-78. Ap. '53. It did happen at Rutgers.

Educational Record. 34:359-70. O. '53. It also happened at Harvard.

*Freeman. 3:50-2. O. 20, '52. Our left-handed colleges: refutes the "liberal" contention that conservatives dominate American colleges. E. M. Root.

Frontier. 3:14-15. Ag. '52. The decline and fall of the fifth amendment. J. W. Caughey.

*Frontier. 4:2. Jl. '53. Unhappy decision. Godfrey Lehman.

Frontier. 4:10-11. O. '53. Education is subversive. H. H. Wilson.

Frontier. 4:12-13. O. '53. Committee and the clergy. A. A. Heist.

Harvard Alumni Bulletin. 55:650-4. My. 23, '53. Academic freedom and congressional committees. An exchange of correspondence between R. B. Perry, G. W. Martin, and Bailey Aldrich.

Harvard Alumni Bulletin. 55:662-3+. My. 23, '53. The corporation statement.

Harvard Alumni Bulletin. 55:690-2+. Je. 6, '53. Press comments on the corporation decision.

*Harvard Crimson. p M1-12. Je. 10, '53. Academic freedom; fifth annual Crimson report.

*Harvard Law Review. 66:1-27. N. '52. New encroachments on individual freedom. J. L. O'Brian.

Harvard Law Review. 66:111-12. N. '52. The Supreme Court, 1951 term: state loyalty programs.

Higher Education. 8:193-6. My. 1, '52. Supreme Court upholds Feinberg Law. J. B. Sanders.

Iowa Law Review. 37:153-74. Winter '52. Law and loyalty. O. K. Fraenkel.

Library Journal. 77:1250-4. Ag. '52. Fight for freedom. R. E. Long.

Life. 34:30. Mr. 9, '53. That campus witch hunt.

Life. 34:90-2+. Je. 22, '53. Is academic freedom in danger? W. Chambers.

　　　Same abridged. Reader's Digest. 63:29-33. S. '53.

Mademoiselle. 37:314. Ag. '53. Meaning of academic freedom. S. A. Wolpert.

Nation. 174:243-4. Mr. 15, '52. Communism in the schools; Feinberg law. Freda Kirchwey.

Nation. 174:658-61. Je. 28, '52. Academic freedom and American society. H. H. Wilson.

Nation. 175:220. S. 13, '52. Teacher's testament. H. F. Stevens.

Nation. 175:310-11. O. 4, '52. What about tomorrow? A. C. Hollingswerth.

Nation. 175:377-8. O. 25, '52. California's crisis in freedom. Eason Monroe.

Nation. 175:568. D. 13, '52. At one college: a daring idea. Broadus Mitchell.

Nation. 175:591-2. D. 27, '52. Cold war and hot emotions; Oklahoma's loyalty oath.

Nation. 175:603-5. D. 27, '52. How to traduce teachers. Broadus Mitchell.

Nation. 176:78. Ja. 24, '53. Giving wolves an appetite. Elmer Davis.

Nation. 176:179. F. 28, '53. Colorado bucks the tide.

Nation. 176:322-4. Ap. 18, '53. Congress on the campus. Alan Barth.

　　　Abridgment of an address delivered before the annual meeting of the AAUP in Chicago.

*Nation. 176:412-14. My. 16, '53. Teacher as rebel: his war for freedom. H. K. Beale.

Nation. 176:433-5. My. 23, '53. Republic of learning; danger from within. Scott Buchanan.

Nation. 176:471-7. Je. 6, '53. Does silence mean guilt? Norman Redlich and L. B. Frantz.

*Nation. 177:265-7. O. 3, '53. Citizen and school, freedom for teachers. H. A. Taylor.

National Education Association Journal. 41:411. O. '52. Intimidating teachers. M. Lindsay.

National Education Association Journal. 42:41. Ja. '53. Scholars must not be shackled; editorial in Illinois State Journal.

*National Education Association Journal. 42:68. F. '53. Oklahoma oath held unconstitutional.

National Education Association Journal. 42:131. Mr. '53. Oregon Legion opposes harassment of educators.

*National Education Association Journal. 42:152-4+. Mr. '53. Intellectual iron curtain. F. H. Horn.

National Education Association Journal. 42:421-2. O. '53. Freedom to learn and freedom to teach; statement by the National Council for the Social Studies.

*National Education Association News. 7:1-8. F. 27, '53. Freedom of the mind. A. E. Meyer.
Same. National Education Association Journal. 42:207-10. Ap. '53.

National Education Association News. 7:1-4. Ap. 10, '53. Tennessee investigates teachers and textbooks.

Nation's Schools. 51:47-50. Ap. '53. Public opinion will judge congressional probes into education. R. A. Skaife.

Nation's Schools. 51:102. Ap. '53. Clergy and labor speak up.

Nation's Schools. 51:110. Ap. '53. Investigations are essential in democracy, says Senator Morse.

Nation's Schools. 51:126. Ap. '53. Conference on higher education urges curbs on congressional investigating committees.

Nation's Schools. 51:47-8. My. '53. This question of subversives. C. O. Johnson.

*New Leader. p s1-15. Ap. 6, '53. Freedom in American culture. Sidney Hook.
Special supplement.

New Republic. 126:17-18. Ja. 21, '52. Loyalty, security and freedom. David Spitz.

New Republic. 126:11-13. F. 4, '52. Loyalty needs better friends. A. P. Davies.

New Republic. 127:20-1. O. 20, '52. Faith in the free mind; excerpt from address, Madison, October 7, 1952. A. E. Stevenson.

New Republic. 128:5-6. Ja. 19, '53. Goose step, 1953.

New Republic. 128:9-10. Ja. 19, '53. Teachers in the toils. Broadus Mitchell.

New Republic. 128:5-6. Mr. 9, '53. Conformity versus freedom.

*New Republic. 128:10-11. Mr. 9, '53. Education and the free-mind principle. A. P. Davies.

New Republic. 128:8. Ap. 13, '53. Loyalty in Pennsylvania.

*New York Herald Tribune. p5. Je. 21, '53. Red probes and Professor X.

New York Times. p 12. F. 18, '52. Text of Yale report on intellectual policy; report issued on Yale University Advisory Committee's survey of 'The Intellectual and Spiritual Welfare of the University, Its Students, and Its Faculty.'

New York Times. p E6. F. 24, '52. House un-American group changes but never quits. C. P. Trussell.

*New York Times. p E10. O. 19, '52. California's loyalty oath.

New York Times. p E8. O. 26, '52. Loyalty of teachers. Leopold Kohr.

*New York Times. p E7. D. 21, '52. Education in review: Supreme Court decision renews controversy over loyalty oaths for teachers. Benjamin Fine.

New York Times. p20. Ja. 5, '53. Against academic restraints. C. C. Burlingham.

New York Times. p 18. Ja. 26, '53. Dr. Conant on communism.

New York Times. p E8. F. 1, '53. Investigating colleges. Peter Gay.

*New York Times. p E8. F. 8, '53. School probe upheld. Norman Thomas.

New York Times. p 10. F. 19, '53. Inquiry on college Reds starts, ignoring protests.

New York Times. p 10. F. 19, '53. U. S. asked to keep hands off schools. Benjamin Fine.

New York Times. p E8. F. 22, '53. Politics of teachers. John Hanna.

New York Times. p E9. F. 22, '53. Schools and colleges strongly object to being investigated by congressmen. Benjamin Fine.

New York Times. p 12. Mr. 12, '53. Colorado ousts eight professors.

New York Times. p 13. Mr. 12, '53. Text of a policy statement on congressional investigations of communism in education adopted by the general board of the National Council of the Churches of Christ in the U. S. A., March 11, 1953.

New York Times. p E8. Mr. 15, '53. Student view on inquiry. P. D. Sheats.

New York Times. p E 13. Mr. 29, '53. City teachers are told that they should not be disturbed by Communist investigations. Benjamin Fine.

New York Times. p 12. Ap. 7, '53. Red inquiry found fifty-four balky teachers.

New York Times. p 16. Ap. 11, '53. Investigating education. Irwin Stark.

New York Times. p E 10. Ap. 26, '53. Limiting inquiries. H. P. Van Dusen.

*New York Times. p26. Ap. 28, '53. Issues in college inquiry. R. B. Perry.

New York Times. p 12. My. 1, '53. NYU professor tied to Reds is dismissed.

New York Times. p 10. My. 5, '53. Pennsylvania's oath upheld reluctantly.

New York Times. p28. My. 5, '53. Loyalty to country and government. Broadus Mitchell.

New York Times. p34. My. 9, '53. Kirk says Columbia maps no Red inquiry.

New York Times. p20. My. 19, '53. Coast plan to ban school Reds cited. C. P. Trussell.

New York Times. p 11. My. 20, '53. Harvard retains three silent at inquiries.

New York Times. p 11. My. 20, '53. Undercover agents denied.

New York Times. p 12. My. 20, '53. University states policy.

*New York Times. p34. Je. 3, '53. Address by Dr. Grayson Kirk, president of Columbia University.
    Same with title Academic freedom is only for free men. Vital Speeches of the Day. 19:557-9. Jl. 1, '53.

New York Times. p20. Je. 16, '53. Address by A. H. Sulzberger before the graduating class of John Carroll University in Cleveland, Ohio.

New York Times. p 17. Je. 17, '53. Senators curtail Red teacher hunt. C. P. Trussell.

*New York Times. p E 10. Jl. 19, '53. Freedom to teach; letter to the editor. G. S. Counts, P. R. Hays, Sidney Hook, A. O. Lovejoy (Commission on Academic Freedom, American Committee for Cultural Freedom).

*New York Times. p E8. O. 18, '53. To protect education. Emile Caillet.

New York Times Magazine. p 12. F. 15, '53. Have we the courage to be free? A. H. Sulzberger.

*New York Times Magazine. p 12+. Ap. 12, '53. Freedom to search for knowledge. R. M. MacIver.

New York Times Magazine. p9+. N. 1, '53. Fifth amendment, a moral issue. Sidney Hook.

New York Times Magazine. p 13+. N. 8, '53. Guilt and innocence by association. H. S. Commager.

Newsweek. 40:37. O. 27, '52. California's oath.

Newsweek. 41:82-3. Mr. 2, '53. Inquiry war.

Newsweek. 42:56. Jl. 13, '53. National Education Association protest.

*Ohio State University Monthly. 44:6-9. Ap. 15, '53. Darkened door.

*Ohio State University Monthly. 44:6-10. My. 15, '53. Darling case.

*Phi Delta Kappan. 24:398-400. Je. '53. Academic freedom and politics. Walton Manning.

*Philadelphia Inquirer. p 14. Mr. 22, '53. They're not bigger than the United States.

Progressive. 17:22-4. Je. '53. The universities surrender. Milton Mayer.

Saturday Evening Post. 225:10+. S. 27, '52. Liberals fleeing with terror; but they still write! Eugene Lyons.

Saturday Evening Post. 225:12. Ap. 18, '53. Academic freedom is not a device to conceal the facts on communism.

Saturday Review. 35:24. O. 25, '52. Equilibrium of freedoms. Harrison Smith.

Saturday Review. 36:14-15. Ap. 4, '53. Colleges for citizens. H. H. Hatcher.

Saturday Review. 36:11-12+. Ap. 18, '53. Can we trust our teachers? Sidney Hook.

*Saturday Review. 36:22-3. S. 26, '53. Should teachers testify? B. F. Wright.

School and Society. 75:8-9. Ja. 5, '52. Loyalty oaths and communistic influences in Negro colleges and universities. R. G. Lloyd.

School and Society. 75:81-4. F. 9, '52. Pechan bill: an asafetida bag for Pennsylvania. H. E. Seyler.

School and Society. 75:137-8. Mr. 1, '52. Academic freedom reasserted at Yale University and Oberlin College; with editorial comment.

School and Society. 76:298. N. 8, '52. Education cannot thrive on fear and suspicion; implementing the Feinberg act. I. L. Kandel.

School and Society. 77:161-4, 171. Mr. 14, '53. Investigate-the-colleges proposals; with editorial comment. H. N. Heston.

School and Society. 77:209-12. Ap. 4, '53. Moral obligations of American colleges. Warren Taylor.

School and Society. 78:11. Jl. 11, '53. Statement on academic freedom in relation to legislative investigations of colleges and universities adopted by the faculty of political science of Columbia University.

School Life. 34:132-4+. Je. '52. Recent Supreme Court decision upholds Feinberg law of New York.

School Life. 35:inside cover. D. '52. Freedom in our classrooms; excerpt from address, October 12, 1952. E. J. McGrath.

Science. 117:647-8. Je. 12, '53. Harvard and the fifth amendment.

Science News Letter. 62:164. S. 13, '52. Loyalty oaths lashed.

Senior Scholastic. 62:14-16. Ap. 15, '53. Congressional investigations, trials or inquiries?

Senior Scholastic. 63:16-17. N. 4, '53. Education, for us or against us?

*Social Education. 16:309-11. N. '52. Recent Supreme Court decisions: the state, the teacher and subversive activity. Isadore Starr.

Southwest Review. 38:296-309. Autumn '53. Education on the razor's edge. H. M. Wriston.

Time. 60:69. S. 22, '52. Communists in the schools.

Time. 60:55. O. 6, '52. Brother, you don't resign; investigating communism in U. S. schools.

Time. 60:13. D. 29, '52. Loyalty decision.

Time. 61:69. F. 23, '53. Search for campus subversives.

Time. 61:53. Ap. 6, '53. Communism and the colleges; excerpt from Rights and responsibilities of universities and their faculties [statement by the Association of American Universities].

*Time. 61:85-6+. Ap. 13, '53. Danger signals; congressional investigations.

Town Meeting (Bulletin of America's Town Meeting of the Air). 18, no42:1-14. Mr. 10, '53. Who should judge the fitness of our college teachers? Carrol Kearns; Eugene McCarthy.

Town Meeting (Bulletin of America's Town Meeting of the Air). 19, no9:3-14. Je. 30, '53. Is the fifth amendment being misused? Norman Redlich; Robert Morris.

United States News & World Report. 35:28-31. S. 11, '53. Mr. Nixon attacks Communist conspirators; excerpts from an address of Vice President Richard M. Nixon before the annual national convention of the American Legion in St. Louis, August 31, 1953.

United States News & World Report. 34:65-7. Ap. 10, '53. Policy of colleges toward Communist teachers; statement issued by Association of American Universities.
    Same. New York Times. p 12. Mr. 31, 53; *same with title* Universities and their faculties. Bulletin of the Atomic Scientists. 9:188-90. Je. '53.

University of Chicago Magazine. 45:5-9. My. '53. A short step to thought control. Laird Bell.

University of Chicago Magazine. 45:5-8. Je. '53. A report on the university of utopia. R. M. Hutchins.

*University of Pennsylvania Law Review. 101:480-508. Ja. '53. A report on the Pennsylvania loyalty act. Clark Byse.

University of Pittsburgh Law Review. 14:90-102. Fall '52. Pennsylvania loyalty act. J. M. Patton.

University Quarterly. 7:348-53. Ag. '53. The Supreme Court of the United States and academic freedom. J. L. Montrose.

Vital Speeches of the Day. 18:162-6. Ja. 1, '52. Personal freedom. P. L. Graham.

Vital Speeches of the Day. 19:69-72. N. 15, '52. Shall human freedom survive? J. G. Diefenbaker.

Vital Speeches of the Day. 19:185-9. Ja. 1, '53. Communism and education. W. F. Russell.

Vital Speeches of the Day. 19:403-6. Ap. 15, '53. Every teacher informed and free. W. G. Carleton.

Vital Speeches of the Day. 19:539-41. Je. 15, '53. The climate of current investigations of communism. G. F. Kennan.

Washington Alumnus. 43:7. Summer '53. Question of academic freedom and responsibility; report of a faculty committee on appointment policies and procedures, University of Washington.

*Washington University Student Life. 74:18+. F. 20, '53. University must stand firm against attacks on liberty. T. C. Hennings.

Yale Review. 42:496-512. Summer '53. National security and individual freedom. R. K. Carr.

Speech and Debating

Competitive Debate: Rules and Strategy. By G. M. Musgrave. 151p. rev. ed. 1946. $1.25.

Democracy Through Discussion. By Bruno Lasker. 376p. 1949. $3.50.

Discussion Methods: Explained and Illustrated. By J. V. Garland. 376p. 3d ed. rev. 1951. $3.

Extempore Speaking: A Handbook for the Student, the Coach, and the Judge. By D. L. Holley. 115p. 1947. $1.50.

High School Forensics: An Integrated Program. By A. E. Melzer. 153p. 1946. 90c.

How to Debate. By H. B. Summers, F. L. Whan, and T. A. Rousse. rev. ed. 349p. 1950. $2.75.

Representative American Speeches. By A. C. Baird, comp. Published annually in The Reference Shelf. Prices vary.

Each volume contains representative speeches by eminent men and women on public occasions during the year. Each speech is prefaced by a short sketch of the speaker and the occasion.

Selected Readings in Rhetoric and Public Speaking. By Lester Thonssen, comp. 324p. 1942. $3.50.